Cambridge English

Niki Joseph

Series Editor: Annette Capel

Prepare!

WORKBOOK

Level 4

Cambridge University Press
www.cambridge.org/elt

Cambridge English Language Assessment
www.cambridgeenglish.org

Information on this title: www.cambridge.org/9780521180283

© Cambridge University Press and UCLES 2015

First published 2015
20 19 18 17 16 15 14 13

Printed in Dubai by Oriental Press

A catalogue record for this publication is available from the British Library

ISBN 978-0-521-18027-6 Student's Book
ISBN 978-1-107-49785-6 Student's Book and Online Workbook
ISBN 978-0-521-18028-3 Workbook with Audio
ISBN 978-0-521-18029-0 Teacher's Book with DVD and Teacher's Resources Online
ISBN 978-0-521-18030-6 Class Audio CDs
ISBN 978-1-107-49782-5 Presentation Plus DVD-ROM

Downloadable audio for this publication at www.cambridge.org/PrepareAudio

Contents

VOCABULARY   Describing people

1 Write the letters in the correct order to make words to describe people (1–6). Then match the opposites (a–f).

1 REINLYFD   ....   a polite
2 RECUAFL   ....   b cheerful
3 DURE   ....   c careless
4 DENONCFIT   ....   d unfriendly
5 UNFNY   ....   e shy
6 SEMIRALEB   ....   f serious

2 Choose the correct adjective.

1 Mark never knows where things are – he loses most of them.   c..............................
2 The woman in the shop said some horrible things.   r..............................
3 What a lovely girl! She's always smiling and so nice.   c..............................
4 Mark's older brother isn't very kind to us when we go to his home.   u..............................
5 Carly never talks to people she doesn't know at parties.   s..............................
6 Emma feels very unhappy because she doesn't like her new school.   m..............................
7 Mum likes you because you say please and thank you!   p..............................
8 When I study I concentrate so I don't make mistakes.   c..............................

3 Complete the crossword, using the clues below.

Across

4 making you laugh or smile
5 behaving in a way that upsets other people
7 describing someone who doesn't laugh very much
9 very sad
10 happy and positive
11 behaving in a pleasant way towards others

Down

1 not happy about talking to new people
2 not kind towards other people
3 not thinking enough about what you are doing
4 behaving in a kind and pleasant way
6 certain about your ability to do things well
8 thinking about what you are doing so you don't make mistakes

4 Look at the pictures and choose the correct word to complete the description.

| attractive   bald   curly   dark   fair   good-looking   straight   teenage   thirties |

a Jenny is in her [1]............................. . She has long dark [2]............................. hair. She's an [3]............................. woman.
b Maggie is a [4]............................. girl. She's got [5]............................. hair too, but it's [6]............................. .
c Bobbie is in his fifties and is [7]............................. .
d Freddie has got short [8]............................. hair. He's [9]............................. .

READING

1 Read this text about birth order. Complete the spaces (1–4) with the words in the box.

eldest child   middle child
only child   youngest child

BIRTH ORDER

Are you an only child? Are you the eldest child? Or the baby of the family? According to some people, your position in your family can change the kind of person you are.

1 ....

You are often very careful because you want to do everything right. You were first, so you are the example! You like doing your homework, you like making lists and you like planning. You don't like anything unexpected. (unless you arrange it) and you want to make people happy, so it can be hard for you to say no.

2 ....

You consider other people's feelings and you hate it when people don't agree with each other. You like it best when everyone is happy. You're friends with all your brothers' and sisters' friends – both older and younger. You can be really funny, too.

3 ....

You never do anything wrong! You are the baby of the family and everyone loves you! You want everyone to watch you. You love people and people love you! For a job, you would be good at selling things. Oh! And you love surprises!

4 ....

By the age of seven, you were already an adult. You've always had adults, not children your own age, in your life. You're good at everything you do. You love reading and you have a clear view of the world. Your favourite word is 'very'. You hate it when you don't succeed. You prefer being with people who are older or younger than yourself – not the same age.

2 Read the text again. Which child …

1 likes studying? ....
2 makes people laugh? ....
3 likes attention from other people? ....
4 enjoys being with adults? ....
5 dislikes things that are not planned? ....
6 always wants to win? ....
7 is liked by everyone in the family? ....
8 likes reading? ....

3 Which 'child' do you think wrote these comments?

1 ....

I'm just like that. I hate birthdays for that reason – you never know if someone is going to suddenly do something that you didn't know about. I hate that.
Judith, Indonesia

2 ....

I don't know. I mean I haven't got any brothers or sisters but I've got a lot of cousins. I don't think that these things are always correct. I don't think they're true!
Cim, Turkey

3 ....

This one is sort of right – I mean, I have got a lot of friends, and people laugh with me at my jokes. But I don't really mind if people are unhappy – you can't be happy all the time!
Zé Miguel, Portugal

4 ....

I hate it when they say things like this! It's just not true! I'm not a baby! Grrrr!
Nini, Peru

4 Match the highlighted words in the text to their meanings.

1 certain or obvious ....
2 events that you didn't expect to happen ....
3 think carefully about something ....
4 plan something for the future ....

EP **Word profile** *right*

Write the words in the correct order to make sentences with *right*.

1 right / me / Mikaela / sitting / to / next / is
....
2 right / sure / you / strange – / you're / That's / are?
....
3 right / is / James / now / so / later / eating / you / can / call back?
....
4 right / finish / We / can / away / this
....
5 right / this / Milton / Is / train / the / for?
....
6 right / turn / to / street / Go / end / the / of / the / and
....

GRAMMAR Present simple and continuous

1 Complete the sentences with the correct form of the verbs in brackets.

1 Julia .... every day at 7 am. (get up)
2 At the moment, my parents .... a TV show on their computer. (watch)
3 Martin .... his new trainers. They're really nice! (wear)
4 We .... our homework in our rooms. (finish)
5 Every day my Dad .... 5 km before work. (run)
6 After lunch on Saturday, I .... my best friend. (visit)

2 Match the questions and the answers.

1 What is Billy doing? ....
2 Do you do anything on Fridays? ....
3 Who plays the piano in your family? ....
4 What are you doing? ....
5 Are you busy next Saturday? ....
6 What time does your school start? ....

a Yes, we usually go shopping.
b That's mum. Jack plays the guitar.
c I'm finishing this exercise.
d Not sure – I usually play basketball with Jo.
e Right now he's playing on his tablet.
f At 9 am every day.

3 Complete the sentences with the words in the box.

> at the moment   every year   later today
> on Mondays   next month   never   right now
> sometimes   this term   tomorrow

1 .... my birthday is on a different day!
2 We're learning about plant life in biology ....
3 .... we're spending two weeks by the sea – it's holiday time!
4 We're visiting my aunt in hospital .... – she had an accident yesterday.
5 I have music practice after school .... so I always get home late.
6 .... I'm doing this exercise!
7 I .... go to bed at 8.30 pm.
8 I have an exam .... so I'm going to bed early tonight.
9 My sister .... goes running before school, but not today – it's raining!
10 Alice can't answer the phone .... – she's having a shower.

4 🔾 Correct the mistakes in these sentences or tick (✔) any you think are correct.

1 When we are together we are having fun.
....
2 I write to tell you that I bought a new computer.
....
3 I send you this email to invite you to my birthday party on Saturday.
....
4 We go out together every week.
....
5 We are best friends and we are playing in the same basketball team.
....

VOCABULARY Verbs: *want, like, love, know*

1 Complete the words with the missing vowels (A, E, I, O, U).

1 B ... L .... V ...
2 H ... T ...
3 KN ... W
4 L ... K ...
5 L ... V ...
6 M .... N
7 N .... D
8 ... WN
9 PR ... F ... R
10 ... ND ... RST ... ND
11 W ... NT

2 Complete the sentences with the positive or negative form of the verbs from exercise 1. You do not need all the verbs. Sometimes more than one answer is possible.

1 I .... your dress – it's so pretty!
2 My aunt .... a house in the mountains – we go there on holiday.
3 I .... this exercise! It's really hard!
4 I .... this book – it's boring.
5 Jack .... to go to basketball now – can you get yourself something to eat?
6 My parents .... my music – but that's OK – I listen with my headphones!
7 Jacki is the kind of girl who .... everything you tell her.
8 Dad .... it when I don't go out on a Saturday night.
9 This sentence is difficult – what do you think it .... ?
10 Mum really .... to go to Italy on holiday, but Dad doesn't so I don't think we'll go.

WRITING   An article

See Prepare to write box, Student's Book page 13.

1 Read the title of the magazine article. Tick (✔) the information you think people will include.

1 age of brothers/sisters ☐
2 parents' jobs ☐
3 where you live ☐
4 favourite food ☐
5 things you do as a family ☐
6 friends' hobbies ☐

Family! Everyone has one!

**What's yours like?
Write in and tell us!**

Your Comments: [2 replies]

I live with my Mum and Dad and my younger sister. She's 5 years old and is really funny!

We're British but Dad is from Australia and we're living in New Zealand at the moment. Mum's a teacher and so she works in different places. It's cool because we travel with her. Dad works with computers and he works from home.

On Saturday mornings we always have breakfast at a café – it's really nice! It's fun family time!

Jamie, aged 14 years, Wellington NZ

Hey!

I'm Sophie and I live with my Mum and Dad and two brothers in Canada. They're both 17. I was born here but my Mum and Dad are English. Dad works for a big company and Mum looks after the home. When we get home, she helps us with our homework and makes dinner. We usually have dinner together but we all do different activities.

One Sunday every month, we go somewhere together. I like that – especially when I can choose!

I love my family!

Sophie, aged 13 years, Edmonton, Canada

2 Read the two magazine articles. Decide who does the following things. Write *Jamie* or *Sophie*. Who …

1 lives in a different place to where they were born? ....
2 has a family that does different things during the week? ....
3 has older brothers? ....
4 eats a meal out with their family every week? ....
5 chooses an activity to do with their family? ....
6 lives in different countries? ....

3 Write some information about yourself for these topics.

What is your name? ....
Who do you live with? ....
Where do you live? ....
What do your mum and dad do? ....
What activities do you do with your family? ....
Where and when do you do them? ....

4 Now using your notes, write a short paragraph about yourself.

• Write about 70 words.
• Remember to check your spelling and grammar.

2 In fashion

VOCABULARY Things to wear

1 Find sixteen clothes words in the word square
(→ ↓), using the clues below.

1 You wear this when it's cold in winter.
2 You put things in this.
3 You wear these on your feet in summer.
4 You wear this when it rains.
5 You wear these over your eyes when it's sunny.
6 People in business wear this.
7 Men wear this around their neck.
8 You wear these when you go for a long walk.
9 Women wear these on their legs.
10 A t-shirt is one of these.
11 You wear this on your head.
12 Something pretty you wear around your neck
13 This is a short coat.
14 Many people wear this with jeans. Some have
   words on the front.
15 You wear these on your feet for sport, or every day.
16 People wear this for sport. It has a top and a
   bottom part.

F	M	C	D	R	X	T	B	Z	T	J	P
K	R	A	X	S	U	I	T	K	O	U	K
T	S	P	N	W	W	E	L	P	P	M	H
P	U	N	T	I	G	H	T	S	W	P	Y
O	N	Q	K	Z	C	R	K	Z	B	E	N
C	G	C	T	J	A	C	K	E	T	R	S
K	L	T	R	A	I	N	E	R	S	Q	A
E	A	T	R	A	C	K	S	U	I	T	N
T	S	W	E	A	T	S	H	I	R	T	D
L	S	B	Z	L	B	O	O	T	S	V	A
F	E	P	R	A	I	N	C	O	A	T	L
T	S	R	N	E	C	K	L	A	C	E	S

2 Match the words to their meanings.

1 loose	....	**a** not wide
2 comfortable	....	**b** wearing attractive, good-quality clothes
3 smart	....	
4 narrow	....	**c** large and comfortable to wear
5 brand-new	....	**d** gives a pleasant feeling
6 fashionable	....	**e** having a clean, tidy and stylish appearance
7 well-dressed	....	**f** completely new
		g popular at a particular time

3 Complete the conversation with the words in the box.

> brand-new   comfortable   raincoat   sunglasses
> smart   tracksuit   tie   well-dressed

A: Have you got your clothes ready for the family weekend away?

B: No, I don't know what to take. Are you taking your ¹............................. ?

A: No! We're not playing sports! Goodness no! I just bought a ²............................. pair of ³............................. – just to give you an idea!

B: What? It's going to rain! I'm taking a ⁴............................. , for sure. We always go outdoors anyhow.

A: I know, but we have a meal on Saturday evening and Mum wants us to look ⁵............................. , you know, her beautiful family. Dad's wearing a ⁶............................. .

B: Really? Well, I want to take ⁷............................. clothes.

A: Hmm, I think Mum wants us to be ⁸............................. actually!

B: I don't care. I'm wearing the clothes I like and that's it.

A: Whatever!

4 Where are the people in exercise 3 going?

1 a camping trip

2 a school sports weekend

3 a family party

READING

1 **Match the words to the picture.**

a **b** **c**

1 trainers ....
2 sandals ....
3 heels ....

2 **Look at the text before reading it. Tick (✔) where it comes from.**

1 a blog ☐ 2 an email ☐ 3 a teen magazine ☐ 4 an online forum ☐

3 **Read the article. Are these sentences true (T) or false (F)?**

1 Many readers bought expensive shoes. ....
2 At Raffi's school, everyone wears the same colour trousers/skirt. ....
3 Raffi wears the same shoes as his friends. ....
4 Anne Belle wrote her name on her trainers. ....
5 At Kat's school, her classmates wear stylish shoes. ....
6 Kat admires her art teacher's style. ....

What do you think about ... shoes?

Most of us wear shoes every day. They protect *our feet from the things we do every day – walking, school, sports and so on. But for some people they are more than that. They follow shoe styles, and a good pair of fashionable shoes – trainers, sandals, or regular shoes – will not be cheap.* **Magaboutyou** *did a survey and we discovered that many of you pay a lot of money for shoes. We think it's because they are an* essential *fashion item – for guys and gals! A pair of shoes can make or break your style!*

Next week: What do you think about ... school bags?

Click here to answer our questions.

Here are some of the comments from the survey.

I think it's silly the way everyone in my school wears the same shoes. We don't have a uniform but the girls all wear the same black trainers. There is one girl in my class who wears different things – but she isn't fashionable, in my opinion. My friends and I wear comfortable trainers and yes, maybe they are all from the same shop. But we like them!
Raffi, South Africa.

I love shoes, especially trainers. They are fashionable and comfortable. You can wear them with everything – trousers, skirts and so on. At school we did a project where we had to add something to a pair of white trainers. I wrote half my name on the left, and the other half on the right. It was such a cool project!
Anne Belle, New Caledonia.

At my school we all have to wear black or brown shoes. It's silly because they are really unfashionable. Nobody likes them. The teachers say they are good shoes for school, but they don't wear them! Our art teacher has a great collection of shoes and in the summer, her sandals are always so pretty. She's really well dressed. I want to dress like her.
Kat, Turkey.

---

4 **Match the highlighted words in the article to their meanings.**

1 protect ....
2 comment ....
3 collection ....
4 essential ....

a something that you say or write that expresses your opinion
b a group of things or people
c very important and necessary
d to keep someone or something safe from something dangerous or bad

5 **Complete the sentences with the correct form of the words from exercise 4.**

1 My raincoat .... me against the rain.
2 Post a .... about my photo.
3 A hat is .... if you play sport in the sun.
4 Phil's dad has an amazing .... of ties.

EP **Word profile** *kind*

Complete the sentences using a suitable phrase with *kind*.

1 My friend and I like the .... of clothes.
2 Susie's got lots of things from Ireland – postcards, guidebooks, ...
3 There are all .... T-shirts in the market and they're very cheap.
4 I'd like to find .... of jewellery-making course if possible.
5 Which .... chocolate do you like best?
6 Thank you for your help – you're very ....

GRAMMAR Past simple

1 Complete the sentences with the verbs in brackets in the past simple.

1 Yesterday I .... my new jacket to school. (wear)

2 Everyone .... the football match last night on TV. (watch)

3 Mum .... to phone her friend, Bess. (forget)

4 Dad .... into town to get Mum's birthday present. (go)

5 Lots of my friends .... their tickets online. (buy)

6 Emily .... off her horse last week. (fall)

7 You .... Mac about football practice last week. (text)

8 We .... you at the party last week. (see)

9 Andrew .... a new bike for his birthday. (get)

10 My brother .... tennis for three hours yesterday. (play)

2 Write the questions for these answers.

1 what / you / do?

....

I went to the cinema with my friend.

2 your dad / drive / his new car?

....

No, he didn't. We went by bus.

3 go / cinema / with parents?

....

No, my parents visited their friends.

4 did / buy / sweets?

....

I did! Three big bags!

5 how long / film / last?

....

About two hours, I think.

6 eat / restaurant / after the film?

....

Yes, we did. We had burgers and salad.

7 you / get home / late?

....

No, we didn't. I think we got home at 8.30 pm.

8 Your parents / come home / later?

....

Yes, they came home around 10 pm.

9 What / you / do / then?

....

I told them about the film.

3 Complete the sentences. Put the verbs into the correct positive or negative form.

1 It was raining so I .... my umbrella. (take)

2 The book was boring and I .... it at all. (enjoy)

3 We .... to Spain for our holidays from London airport. (fly)

4 My best friend .... me a lovely birthday present. (give)

5 Suni .... to play with Marta because he was watching TV. (want)

6 It was a hot day and we .... lots of water. (drink)

7 You .... visit me last week because you had to do your homework, remember? (visit)

8 She .... you an email this morning. (send)

4 Complete the text with the verbs in the box. Use the simple past, positive or negative.

ask	catch	drive	go	practise	smile
speak	spend	teach	try	understand	

Eve [1] .... on holiday with her parents last year. They [2] .... a plane from London to Rome, Italy and then [3] .... to a small town nearby. They [4] .... two weeks there. Eve's mum [5] .... her some Italian words and so she [6] .... as often as possible. She [7] .... for food in the restaurant or a café. When people [8] .... to her she [9] .... everything, but she [10] .... and they were pleased that she [11] .... Now Eve wants to study Italian at school.

5 ⊙ Choose the correct sentence in each pair.

1 a We were there for three days because last week is a holiday.

  b We were there for three days because last week was a holiday.

2 a Last Saturday I went with my friends to the cinema.

  b Last Saturday I go with my friends to the cinema.

3 a The National Park is a clean and quiet place, so we chose to go there.

  b The National Park is a clean and quiet place, so we choosed to go there.

4 a She so surprised and really happy!

  b She was so surprised and really happy!

5 a I have a lot of fun last weekend.

  b I had a lot of fun last weekend.

VOCABULARY Adverbs

1 Write the letters in the correct order to make adverbs.

1 GRIYALN ....
2 LABYD ....
3 LRAUYLFCE ....
4 SAFT ....
5 LEWL ....
6 DHAR ....
7 YICQLUK ....
8 WOSLLY ....

2 Complete the sentences with an adverb from exercise 1.

1 That man is driving too f............................. .
2 You made that birthday card really w............................. . Good job!
3 Unfortunately Matt did b............................. in his test – I don't think he studied.
4 The driver shouted a............................. at the boy running across the road.
5 Sheila is working h............................. for her piano exam – she practises every day.
6 Can you run to the shops q............................. and get a packet of biscuits?
7 Mum drove s............................. because it was raining a lot.
8 I c............................. opened the box and saw my present – a puppy!

LISTENING

1 Look at the photo. Where are the teens? Tick (✔) the event where you think they are.

1 a special birthday party ☐
2 an end-of-high school party ☐
3 a wedding party ☐

2 ▶2 Now listen and check your answer.

3 ▶2 Listen again and choose the correct answers.

1 Rob is talking about his *cousin / sister*, Denise.
2 Denise left school *last year / two years ago*.
3 Rob thinks proms are *British / American.*
4 Rob thinks it *is / isn't* a good idea to spend a lot of money on a Prom dress.
5 Denise got a job in a *café / clothes shop*.
6 Lara believes you *have to / don't have to* buy your Prom dress yourself.

4 ▶2 Listen again and complete the first part of the conversation.

Lara: Hey Rob, is that your sister? She's ¹............................. !

Rob: Yeah that's Denise! And that's a ²............................. from last year! Do you ³............................. , Lara, she went to that end-of-year ⁴............................. , the Prom?

Lara: And is that Andy Patterson with her? He's very ⁵............................. , isn't he?

Rob: Yep! In his ⁶............................. tie!

Lara: I can't ⁷............................. till our Prom, can you?

Rob: Do you think I'm going to wear a tie like that?

Lara: Yes, you have to! Everyone does when they ⁸............................. school.

Rob: Hmm. I think the Prom comes from ⁹............................. .

③ My way of life

VOCABULARY   Life events

1 Add the missing vowels (A, E, I, O, U) to complete these life events.

1 B.... B.... RN
2 G....T .... D....GR........
3 G....T .... DR....V....NG L....C....NC....
4 G....T .... J....B
5 H....V.... CH....LDR....N

6 L........V.... H....M....
7 ST....RT SCH........L
8 G....T M....RR........D
9 G.... T.... ....N....V....RS...TY
10 L........V.... SCH........L

2 Look at the pictures. What are they celebrating? Write a life event from exercise 1 in each space.

1 ....   2 ....   3 ....   4 ....   5 ....

3 Complete the sentences with the correct form of the words from exercise 1.

1 I want to .... in London and study history.
2 My sister is going to .... to her boyfriend next year!
3 My Dad .... in the last century.
4 These days many people .... when they are in their 30s or 40s.
5 In my country, all children .... when they are five years old.
6 I want to .... and then buy a second-hand car.
7 My brother .... in physics from New York University last year.
8 My friend's older brother .... as a car mechanic.

4 Match the questions and the answers.

1 What is Charlie going to study at university?   ....   a Definitely not before I am 30!
2 How old are you?   ....   b I was born in 2004.
3 When did you start school?   ....   c He wants to get a degree in English.
4 Do you think you will have children?   ....   d I went to school when I was 6 years old.
5 Is your sister going to leave school next year?   ....   e I don't think so, and anyway she's only 16.

READING

 a    b    c    d

1 Match the cards to the special events.

1 You finish university.   ....
2 It's your birthday.   ....

3 You get your driving licence.   ....
4 You have exams.   ....

2 Read the online comments about cards. Which events from exercise 1 are mentioned?

Do you send cards? Do you receive cards? We asked you to tell us cards you send for special events.

❯ **Carrie:** I enjoy making cards, and I think I'm good at it. It's nicer because you can make it really personal, too. My sister recently got her driving licence and I made a card that looked like a car! I made it out of coloured paper and things I had at home. It's not easy to do but I enjoyed doing it and my sister loved it!

❯ **Stu:** My Grandma sends me a card every year for my birthday with some money in it! So I guess it's good for that! I don't send cards because stamps are really expensive, although I sometimes send a text message or a photo instead. I think cards are only for old people!

❯ **Jon:** I was in a shop yesterday and I bought a great card for my cousin. He got his degree and he's really happy. I don't usually buy cards but this was perfect! It was a funny cartoon. My Mum sometimes sends birthday cards, especially to her sister and family in the USA, and my aunt sends me a card for my birthday. I guess it's just what our family does!

❯ **Chrissie:** I love sending cards. There's a shop in my town that sells only cards. It's wonderful! You can buy cards to celebrate every occasion. But I know that most of my friends don't buy cards. They think they are expensive and they can send a text for nothing. But it's not the same.

3 Read the text. Who …?

1 creates their own cards? ....
2 received a card with cash in it? ....
3 enjoys buying cards? ....
4 receives cards from family in a different country? ....
5 prefers to send text messages? ....
6 gave a funny card? ....

4 Match the highlighted words in the text to their meanings.

1 celebrate ....
2 expensive ....
3 stamp ....
4 cartoon ....
5 occasion ....

a a small piece of paper you buy and put on a letter before sending it.
b a funny drawing, especially in a newspaper or magazine
c do something enjoyable because it's a special day
d a special time
e costing a lot of money

5 Complete the sentences with a word from exercise 4.

1 We went out for dinner to .... my Mum's birthday.
2 This card is very .... – I'm not paying that!
3 I need to put a .... on this letter.
4 My sister drew a funny .... for her art homework.
5 It was a special .... and Mum bought me new clothes.

6 Look at the text in each question. What does it say?

1

Sorry to hear you're still in hospital, Anna. Your mum says you'll be home on Friday, though? I'll definitely come and see you once more before then. Love, Auntie Jean

In this card, Auntie Jean is
A asking Anna to come and see her on Friday.
B promising to visit Anna again in hospital.
C apologising to Anna for not being at home.

2

My class spent the day here. The guided tour was boring, but we all had fun making a 14th-century meal in the castle kitchen. It wasn't nice to eat, though!
Sam

What did Sam enjoy doing at the castle?
A spending time in the café
B going on a guided tour
C preparing some food

EP Word profile get

Complete the sentences with the correct form of *get*.

1 My plane .... in at midnight – can you meet me?
2 Finn didn't .... to the singing class. He's really disappointed.
3 Martha .... with her younger cousins really well.
4 Shirley .... married next summer!
5 Robin .... a new phone yesterday.

GRAMMAR Comparatives and superlatives, *not as … as*

1 How many syllables have the following words got?

1 beautiful .... 3 lovely .... 5 nice ....

2 great .... 4 serious .... 6 typical ....

2 Complete the flow chart with the words in the box.

big bigger expensive greater happier narrower nicer

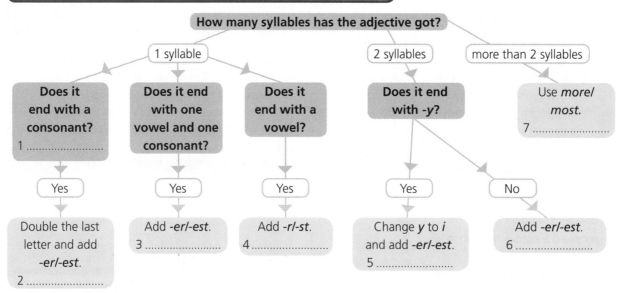

How many syllables has the adjective got?

| 1 syllable | 2 syllables | more than 2 syllables |

Does it end with a consonant?
1 ....

Does it end with one vowel and one consonant?

Does it end with a vowel?

Does it end with -y?

Use *more/most.*
7 ....

Yes — Double the last letter and add *-er/-est*.
2 ....

Yes — Add *-er/-est*.
3 ....

Yes — Add *-r/-st*.
4 ....

Yes — Change *y* to *i* and add *-er/-est*.
5 ....

No — Add *-er/-est*.
6 ....

3 Write the comparative and superlative forms of the following adjectives.

1 heavy ....

2 short ....

3 cheap ....

4 unusual ....

5 miserable ....

6 sunny ....

4 Some words are *irregular*. Complete the table.

	Comparative	Superlative
good	1	2 ....
bad	3	4 ....

5 Complete the sentences with the correct form of the adjectives in brackets.

1 .... place for a holiday is by the beach. (good)

2 Magda got .... mark in the class. (high)

3 This shopping mall is .... than the one in town. I don't like it! (crowded)

4 Eating fruit is .... than eating chocolate. (healthy)

5 This week's homework is .... than last week's. (difficult)

6 Jake's bike was .... of all the bikes outside the house. (dirty)

7 Davy is .... than Frank. (short)

8 Maths is .... subject for me at school – I can't do it at all! (bad)

6 Write the words in the correct order to complete the sentences.

1 Freda's café as / isn't / Mike's / busy / as

....

2 Your house as / isn't / Julie's / as / big

....

3 My trousers / fashionable / aren't / as / my / as / friend's

....

4 Zoe as / as / tall / Louis / isn't

....

5 People say that New York / dangerous / isn't / New Orleans / as / as

....

6 Here in the countryside, / as / as / fast / in / the internet speed isn't / city / the

....

7 👁 Correct the mistakes in these sentences or tick (✔) any you think are correct.

1 My old sister invited her to go out with us.

....

2 My granddad became more happy.

....

3 We go horse riding together but I am not as good as her.

....

4 He's a bit taller and thiner than me.

....

5 We saw the last film with Tom Cruise. I liked it!

....

VOCABULARY *too, not enough*

1 **Rewrite the sentences so that they mean the same. Use *too* or *not enough*.**

1 This bag is too small.

....

2 This jacket isn't loose enough.

....

3 These shoes are too small for me.

....

4 This computer is too slow.

....

5 My Mum's car isn't big enough for our bikes.

....

6 These trousers aren't long enough.

....

2 **Complete the text with *too* or *enough*.**

Yesterday I wanted to go into town. It was
[1] .... far to walk and so I decided to
get the bus. When the bus arrived there wasn't
[2] .... room for me because it was
[3] .... crowded. The bus wasn't big
[4] .... ! So finally I walked into town.

WRITING An informal email

See Prepare to write box, Student's Book page 23.

1 **Look at the picture. Tick (✔) the things you can see.**

1	belt	☐	5 pockets	☐
2	earrings	☐	6 necklace	☐
3	narrow jeans	☐	7 cap	☐
4	curly hair	☐	8 skirt	☐

2 **Read this email and answer the questions.**

Hi Evan!
I hope you're feeling better. It was a pity you
missed Rachel's party last night. It was amazing!
When we arrived, her mum asked us to put our
phones in a box. She said it was a 'no phone'
party. At first nobody liked that, but then it was
OK. It was the best party! Rachel was really happy
because she passed her art exam and she's going
to a different school from the rest of us. It's as
good as our school for most subjects but I think
it's better for art.
The food was great, and Rachel's mum baked the
most delicious bread. It was really good and there
were lots of salads, and pizza too. There was great
music and dancing too! Everyone chatted and we
had a lovely time.
Get better soon!
Marieke

1 Who had the party last night?   ....
2 What did she pass?   ....
3 Why is she going to a new school? ....
4 What did they eat?   ....
5 Did Marieke enjoy the party?   ....

3 **Underline four short forms in Marieke's email.**

4 **Rewrite the sentences using short forms.**

1 He has not got his phone with him.

....

2 She does not know anyone here.

....

3 We are going to leave soon.

....

4 I am bored.

....

5 What is your friend's name?

....

5 **Plan an email to Evan telling him about the boy in the picture. Write down your ideas, using the questions to help you**

• Why was he miserable?

....

• Did he know anyone?

....

• Did he like the food?

....

• Your own ideas.

....

6 **Write your email to Evan.**

• Write about 80–100 words.
• Remember to check your spelling and grammar.

4 Champions

VOCABULARY Sports

1 Write the letters in the correct order to make sports words.

1 HELTTICAS ....
2 HASQUS ....
3 GIGONGJ ....
4 FINUSRG ....

5 NITYSACMSG ....
6 XINBOG ....
7 BLIINCGM ....
8 LYGCCIN ....

2 Match the sports to the pictures.

> ice hockey   climbing   tennis   rugby

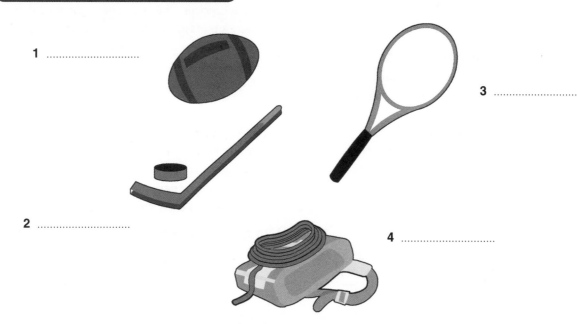

1 ....

3 ....

2 ....

4 ....

3 Write these sports into the correct column in the table. Some may go into more than one column.

> boxing   climbing   swimming   squash
> ice skating   tennis   volleyball   windsurfing

inside	outside	with a ball	without a ball
squash		squash	

4 Complete the sentences with the correct verb: *go, play* or *do*.

1 Do you want to .... basketball after school?
2 My little sister .... gymnastics every Saturday morning – she's getting really good!
3 My friend .... ice hockey at the sports centre on Wednesdays.
4 Elise wants to .... ice skating with us.
5 My older brother .... climbing in his free time.
6 Would you like to .... table tennis with us?
7 It rained and so we didn't .... athletics.
8 Let's .... snowboarding in the mountains at the weekend!

READING

Finding out about ... skateboarding for girls

1 Which description matches the picture?

1 We can see a girl skateboarding up something. There are lots of people watching and she's doing really well.

2 We can see a girl skateboarding down something. I'm not sure what it is, but it looks as if it's outside.

3 There's a girl skateboarding. I think she's doing something really difficult on her skateboard. She's inside and the lights are on.

Vic Arucana finds out more about the teen girl skateboarding scene.

Recently I met 25-year-old Elsa Dakota at a skate park in California. Elsa started skateboarding when she was just 12 years old. Her uncle gave her a skateboard as a present. 'I jumped on it at the park with some friends and I knew that's what I wanted to do! I felt so free,' she says. A couple of years later, she was skating in her local park when she saw an advertisement for a competition. She entered and won! 'Then it all happened really fast,' remembers Elsa. 'I became a professional skateboarder at 15! It was a really exciting time for me – you know, more competitions, more training …' Did she have any problems? 'We were good,' says Elsa, 'but it was difficult. As girls, we were trying to join in and do well in something that was mainly for boys, and the boys earned more in prize money. It's different now and girls have their own competitions. It's great!'

Later in the day young **Helene Gallin**, 15, joined us before her lesson with Elsa. What is her opinion on the world of skateboarding for girls? 'It used to be hard,' says Helene, 'but it's better now because it's easy for girls to take part in competitions, and we're encouraged a lot more too. I think a lot of things are easier for girls now.' She continues, 'Nowadays there are even girls-only events and that is a big change! Skateboarding for girls is here to stay.' Go girls!

Next month: bungee jumping – backwards!

2 Read the article and answer the questions.

1 In the past, boys received
   a bigger prizes than girls.
   b less money than girls.

2 Elsa Dakota started skateboarding because
   a a family member gave her a present.
   b her friends invited her to go skateboarding with them.

3 After Elsa won her first competition
   a she started to teach younger children to skateboard.
   b she started to earn money from skateboarding.

4 Why were there difficulties for her?
   a She was doing something that was generally for boys.
   b She hurt herself a lot.

5 What does Helene Gallin think about girls skateboarding?
   a Many girls aren't very keen on skateboarding.
   b It has a future because more girls are taking it up.

6 What big change do Elsa and Helene talk about?
   a There are competitions that are just for girls.
   b More people take part in competitions.

3 Match the highlighted words in the article to their meanings.

1	professional	....	**a** what someone thinks or believes
2	join in	....	**b** something that happens
3	opinion	....	**c** continue to be in a certain way
4	stay	....	**d** become involved in an activity with other people
5	event	....	**e** describes someone who earns money from their sport or activity

EP Word profile *way*

Match the questions and answers.

1	Can we go to Alyssa's? She's got my book.	....	**a** No way! That's far too much!
2	Can I open my eyes?	....	**b** It's a long way away – not till next month!
3	Can you tell me about Japan?	....	**c** It depends – there are many ways!
4	When's your maths test, Charlie?	....	**d** You can do it now or later, but either way you have to do it.
5	Did you return my library books?	....	**e** I did. By the way, did you know Mrs Beaver works there now?
6	How do you cook eggs?	....	**f** Sure, her house is on the way to Uncle Bill's.
7	When do I have to clean my room?	....	**g** Yes, but look the other way. OK. Ready? Surprise!
8	Dad ate four bowls of pasta last night.	....	**h** Yes, we cycled a long way today.
9	Are you tired?	....	**i** Well, the way of life is different to the UK.

GRAMMAR Past continuous

1 **Write the words in the correct order to make sentences.**

1 doing / I / yesterday / was / athletics

....

2 swimming / in / were / boys / The / sea / the

....

3 talking / were / We / the / for / time / long / phone / on / a

....

4 watching / you / TV / Were / ?

....

5 wasn't / in / I / class / texting

....

6 sitting / They / table / weren't / at / our

....

7 you / Were / for / phone / looking / your / ?

....

8 playing / tennis / he / yesterday / Was / ?

....

2 **Complete the sentences with *was, were, wasn't* or *weren't*.**

1 The man .... walking to work because it was a lovely day.

2 What .... you doing? Look!

3 I .... studying really hard last night.

4 The boys .... playing tennis – it was volleyball!

5 .... you watching TV at 8 pm last night?

6 What .... your sister doing at lunchtime?

7 I .... playing on your computer yesterday. I was out on my bike.

8 We .... listening to you – can you say it again please?

3 **Complete the sentences with the past continuous form of the verbs in brackets.**

1 When I came into the kitchen, Jason and Gary .... breakfast together. (cook)

2 While we were at Grandma's, I .... my friend about a party. (text)

3 When I got home, Mum .... an email to my Uncle. (write)

4 I .... a computer game! (not play)

5 We .... at your yellow shorts, honestly! (not laugh)

6 Margot .... a beautiful dress. (wear)

7 .... your homework at 6 pm last night? (do)

8 .... during the storm? (your Dad / drive)

4 **Complete the text with the correct form of the verbs in the box.**

do   draw   play   read
shine   sing   sit   watch

Finish the story.

Yesterday the sun [1] .... and the birds [2] .... I [3] .... outside and I [4] .... a picture. My brother [5] .... in the garden. Mum and Dad [6] .... anything special. I think Mum [7] .... a book and Dad [8] .... TV inside.

What do you think happened next? Finish the story and send it to endthestory@yourstory.com.

5 ⊙ **Choose the correct sentence in each pair.**

1 a On her way back to the hotel she saw a deer that is standing beside the road eating grass.

b On her way back to the hotel she saw a deer that was standing beside the road eating grass.

2 a I was planing to have a picnic on Saturday.

b I was planning to have a picnic on Saturday.

3 a He was playing basketball alone.

b He was play basketball alone.

4 a I first met him at primary school, while we was playing football.

b I first met him at primary school, while we were playing football.

5 a I was studying at her school until last year, but I moved.

b I was studing at her school until last year, but I moved.

VOCABULARY Words with different meanings

1 **Complete the sentences with the correct form of the words in the box. Use each word twice.**

coach   fit   match   point   trainer

1 The .... wants everyone to get to the stadium before 5 pm because the .... leaves at 5 pm.

2 You can't see the colour on these .... and I'm going to buy the same ones that the football club .... has.

3 Our .... is next week – we have to get some shorts that .... our tops.

4 Max .... to the score – we won by one .... !

5 This sweatshirt .... me well, doesn't it? Now I need to do some exercise to get .... !

2 Complete the sentences with the correct form of the words from exercise 1.

1 That skirt doesn't .... – it's too big!
2 Our team won by three .... – 29–26! Hurray!
3 Next week it's the final football .... of this year.
4 Our tennis .... wants us to practise for two hours every day.
5 What colour are your .... ?

LISTENING

1 Read the poster. What does it mean?

1 A new sports centre opened last week.
2 If you go on Saturday, you will have to pay.
3 On Saturday you can try different sports for free.

Opening soon!

Bank Sports Centre

Come along and have a go at some new sports!

Open Day Saturday 9 am – 4 pm

Bring a friend and have fun!

Free entry!

2 ▶3 Listen to the radio podcast. Tick (✔) the information the interviewer asks about.

1 what makes Bank Sports Centre different ☐
2 more information about new sports ☐
3 if there are team sports ☐
4 sports that use a ball ☐
5 summer activities ☐
6 the open day ☐
7 opening times ☐

3 ▶3 Listen again. Are these sentences true (T) or false (F)?

1 There's a gym at the sports centre. ....
2 The room for hot yoga is 44 °C. ....
3 There is a type of yoga you can do in the air. ....
4 In the winter you can do ice skating. ....
5 In the summer, they put sand down for summer sports. ....
6 The open day means only members can go along. ....
7 There will be prizes on Saturday. ....

4 ▶3 Listen again and complete the information.

1	Name of sports centre	....
2	Popular activities	swimming pool, classes and ....
3	Two types of yoga	.... and yoga in the air
4	New winter sports	....
5	New summer sport	....
6	Open day on	on .... from .... am

5 ▶3 Listen again. How did the people say the following?

1 The Bank Sports Centre is similar to all sports centres.
....
2 We want people to try out new activities.
....
3 It's enjoyable.
....
4 What sport can I do, that I haven't done before?
....
5 Bring everyone – any age!
....
6 It doesn't cost any money.
....

5 Take a good look

VOCABULARY People and action verbs

1 Label the picture with the words and phrases in the box.

> catch   clap   drop   fight   hit   hold   make a face   point   shake hands   throw   wave

a ....
b ....
c ....
d ....
e ....
f ....
g ....
h ....
i ....
j ....
k ....

2 Complete the sentences about the picture with the correct form of the verbs from exercise 1.

Look at this picture! It's from the football match last week. There are Billy and Bob who [1] .... as usual. They don't like each other! Oh and this is my Mum. She [2] .... her bag. That little boy there is Jack. He [3] .... up at the plane in the sky. There are Dan and Bruce, the coaches. They [4] .... after the match. Mum and her friend, Lucy, [5] .... because Wesley's team won the match. Those three girls are playing with balls. The tallest one [6] .... a ball and the shortest [7] .... it. Kirie is in the middle and she [8] .... the ball. I think they're having fun!

3 Choose the correct verb.

1 Charlie! *Drop / Throw* me the ball!
2 Luckily, Kyle *caught / dropped* his phone before it broke.
3 Is it polite to *clap / point* at people in your country?
4 The two children were *hitting / fighting*. I told them to stop.
5 I *made / held* a face when you took my photo.
6 My parents *shook / waved* hands with the teacher when they left.

4 Complete the sentences with the correct form of the verbs from exercise 1.

1 I met my mother's friend and we .... hands.
2 Can you see me? I'm .... at you. Look up!
3 Luke fell over and .... his phone. It doesn't work now.
4 My two cats look as if they .... but they're really playing.
5 No, Sophia! Don't .... a face like that. It's not nice.
6 After the wonderful performance, everyone ....
7 Can you help me? This box is very heavy and I can't .... it any longer.
8 Sorry, I didn't mean to .... you on the head! Are you OK?

EP **Word profile** *take*

Match the questions and answers.

1 Can you ride a horse? ....
2 Why is the city so busy? ....
3 Why is Mary on her own? ....
4 Can I stop now? ....
5 Do you know where my phone is? ....
6 What's your number again? ....
7 What do you want to do after lunch? ....
8 Did you give your teacher the project? ....

a OK, take a note. It's 444 666.
b I think Meg took it.
c Let's take a walk.
d Yes, I took it up when I was five.
e Yes, it took me about five hours to finish!
f Sure, take a five-minute break.
g There's an important sports event that is taking place.
h She doesn't want to take part.

READING

1 **Where do you see a *hashtag* (#)?**

1 It's a letter in some languages that means 'not'.
2 You put it before a word in social media to connect it to others.
3 It's used in website addresses which belong to photographers.

2 **Read the article quickly. What is the author doing?**

1 explaining why he wants more followers
2 asking for advice for a friend
3 writing about his friend's experience with a social media site

20m ago

♥ like   ⟷ comment

#monument #me #beautiful #loveholidays #sky #fun

♥ 25 likes

#takephotos #followme #followingyou

Do you take selfies showing yourself pointing at a famous monument and hashtag it #famous #monument #me?

How many followers have you got on social media? Do you know how to increase the number of people who follow you?

#Hashtagging

If you hashtag your photos, you make them more available and that means that people can find them. Also, the hashtag takes you to other photos with the same word. You can also download a hashtag app that creates the hashtags for you – you can write the words yourself, but this is quicker!

My friend Carlos wanted to see how quickly he could get more followers. He downloaded the hashtag app and then took a photo of himself waving at the sun. It's a funny photo! Anyhow, he posted the photo with lots of hashtags. That meant that just about everything in the photo had a hashtag. His photo immediately got more 'likes' than usual. What a great feeling! The next day he took a similar photo but this time he was clapping at the sun. He posted it and hashtagged it. He did this for a few days but his friends found the hashtags were annoying. He had some comments like:

What are you doing? #why?

And then some people stopped following him. That was not the idea! But perhaps his friends just didn't understand what he was doing.

Another way to get more likes and followers is to post a collection of photos. This could be about five different pictures at the same time, or even better, download a photography app and make them into one collage – a picture of pictures. Carlos did this too and his bio included the sentence 'Follow me and I'll follow you back.' Finally he started to get more followers!

What do you do to get more followers?

3 **Choose the best ending for the sentences.**

1 The author's friend wanted to find out more about hashtags and *apps / getting more followers*.
2 Carlos posted a photo of himself *inside / outside* his house.
3 When he added hashtags, he *managed to get more likes / lost some of his friends*.
4 Some of his friends *knew / hated* what he was doing.
5 Carlos began to post *single pictures / groups of pictures*.
6 When people knew he followed them back, they *followed / didn't follow* him.

4 **Match the highlighted words in the text to their meanings.**

1 a group of things ....
2 get bigger or make something bigger ....
3 an old building or place that is important in history ....
4 pictures you take of yourself ....
5 a short few lines about yourself including your name and what you do ....
6 makes something happen ....

GRAMMAR   Past simple and continuous

1 Choose the correct verb forms.

A young woman ¹ *became / was becoming* a local hero yesterday. Shelley O'Reilley ² *worked / was working* at a hairdresser's in New York, USA, when two young men in their mid-twenties ³ *walked / were walking* in. They ⁴ *stole / were stealing* a phone that belonged to a young girl.

Shelley said, 'I ⁵ *was cleaning / cleaned* the floors. They ⁶ *were leaving / left* the hairdresser's and, as they ⁷ *walked / were walking* towards the door, they kept looking back at me.' She ⁸ *guessed / was guessing* what they ⁹ *did / were doing*.

She ¹⁰ *ran / was running* out of the hairdresser's and, as they ¹¹ *got / were getting* into their car, she put her foot in the door so that they couldn't shut it. One of them tried to hit her but then Shelley ¹² *saw / was seeing* a police car. The police quickly ¹³ *stopped / were stopping* the thieves.

2 Choose the best answer in each sentence.

1 What were you doing yesterday at 5 pm?
   a I listened to music and did my homework.
   b I was listening to music and doing my homework.
2 Who were you talking to this morning?
   a My Mum phoned because she wanted me to buy some bread.
   b My Mum was phoning me because she wanted me to buy some bread.
3 What happened to your foot?
   a I was playing football and fell over.
   b I was playing football and was falling over.
4 Did you enjoy the dinner last night?
   a Yes, it was great. I was eating pizza.
   b Yes, it was great. I ate pizza.
5 Did you hear the doorbell?
   a No, I was sleeping.
   b No, I slept.

3 Make sentences using the past simple or past continuous.

1 I / have breakfast / with / my family / at 7 am.
   ....
2 Those boys / take / photos / their pets / for two hours.
   ....
3 Mum / tell / us / a story about / Grandma / when / her phone / ring.
   ....
4 In the picture / the little boy / point at / the plane / in the sky.
   ....
5 Mark / not wave / at Julie / because / not / see her.
   ....
6 You / not wear / a blue T-shirt this morning – / it / red.
   ....

4 Complete the conversation with the past simple or past continuous form of the verbs in the box.

be	get	imagine	look	love
run	see	sing	take	think

A: That's a good photo. Tell me about it!
B: I ¹ .... before school down the road – late as usual! It ² ....
a beautiful day and the birds ³ ....
I ⁴ .... about my English homework. I had to write a story about a photo. I didn't know what to write. You know, when you have no ideas! But then I ⁵ .... up and
I ⁶ .... this amazing hot air balloon above me! I ⁷ .... out my phone and
⁸ .... a photo.
A: Did you write about it for your homework?
B: I did! I ⁹ .... the lives of the people in the balloon. My teacher ¹⁰ ....
the story! I got a great mark!

5 ☉ Correct the mistakes in these sentences or tick (✔) any you think are correct.

1 They played games in the game centre when I saw them.
   ....
2 On Saturday, although it was raining, I went to the fun fair with my friends.
   ....
3 In the evening we were going to cinemas and theatres.
   ....
4 It was summer but it snowed when I woke up.
   ....
5 I arrived home in the morning, then I was sleeping all day.
   ....

VOCABULARY *myself, yourself, each other*

1 **Match the questions and answers.**

1 What happened to Jill's hand? ....
2 Who cut your hair? ....
3 What are those boys doing? ....
4 How was football practice? ....
5 Are you sending Zoe a present? ....

a I did it myself! Do you like it?
b Of course! We always give each other presents on our birthdays!
c They're arguing with each other.
d She burnt herself while she was cooking.
e It was good! We all enjoyed ourselves.

2 **Complete the conversations with the correct pronoun.**

1 **A:** What happened to your arm?
  B: I fell off my bike and hurt ....
2 **A:** Can your Dad speak Spanish?
  B: Yes, a bit. He taught .... last year before our holiday.
3 **A:** What are those girls doing?
  B: Taking photos of ....
4 **A:** I'm thirsty. Can I have a glass of water?
  B: Sure, help ....
5 **A:** Can you sister play the piano?
  B: Yes, she taught............................. ! She's amazing!

WRITING A description

See Prepare to write box, Student's Book page 35.

1 **Look at the pictures and read the text. Which photo is it describing, A or B?**

I took this photo last year. I was on holiday with my parents and we wanted to see whales. So we joined a tour and went out on a boat for the day. I love the sea – it's so beautiful and powerful. There were lots of kids my age and we all wanted to see the whales. We were all looking at the sea when suddenly we heard an enormous splash of water! It was a whale! And then we saw it again! I quickly took out my camera and Snap! I took the photo and I love it! I really enjoyed myself on that holiday.

By Zeynep.

2 **Tick (✔) the topics that Zeynep included.**

1 where she took the photo ☐
2 when she took the photo ☐
3 who she was with ☐
4 where she keeps the photo ☐
5 what the photo is of ☐
6 how she took the photo ☐

3 **Look at these words from exercise 1. Are they adverbs or adjectives? Add two more to each group of your own.**

	adjective	adverb
1 quickly	☐	☐
2 really	☐	☐
3 enormous	☐	☐
4 beautiful	☐	☐
5 powerful	☐	☐
6 suddenly	☐	☐
....	☐	☐
....	☐	☐
....	☐	☐
....	☐	☐

4 **Complete the sentences with an adjective or adverb from exercise 3.**

1 It was a .... , sunny day.
2 It .... started raining.
3 This is a .... camera – it takes great photos.
4 I took this photo .... – it's not very good.
5 My best friend lives in an .... house.
6 This is a .... great picture – I love it!

5 **Read the competition information. You are going to write your own 'Best Holiday photo'.**

PHOTOGRAPHY COMPETITION!

'Best Holidays'
Send us your best holiday photo and tell us why it was special!
Send your photos to photocomp@bestphotsever.com.

- Write why it was special.
- Write about 80–100 words.
- Remember to check your spelling and grammar.

VOCABULARY City life

1 Complete the crossword using the clues below.

Across

1 There was a large .... waiting for the film stars.

4 In London, there is a famous .... over the River Thames that opens.

6 There is so much .... in some cities that you can't see the sun.

7 Here's the .... for paper that you don't want.

8 Let's sit beside the .... – it's lovely to hear the sound of the water.

Down

2 Don't drop your .... – pick it up and take it home!

3 We can leave our car in the .... – it's free on Sundays.

5 Some .... is beautiful and many people think it is art.

2 Match 1–10 with a–j to make compound nouns. There may be more than one possible answer.

1	apartment	....	a	block
2	bus	....	b	crossing
3	car	....	c	jam
4	department	....	d	lights
5	pedestrian	....	e	lights
6	public	....	f	market
7	street	....	g	park
8	street	....	h	stop
9	traffic	....	i	store
10	traffic	....	j	transport

3 Choose the correct answer.

1 Sam and Billy left their car in the car ....
   a stop   **b** transport   **c** park

2 I think we can get over the road here, at the pedestrian ....
   a crossing   **b** lights   **c** stop

3 I don't like driving in the dark – the street .... aren't very bright.
   a market   **b** lights   **c** store

4 We're going to be late – there's a traffic ....
   a lights   **b** park   **c** jam

5 Let's go to the street .... tomorrow and look for presents.
   a lights   **b** market   **c** crossing

6 Is this the bus .... for the number 14 into the city centre?
   a park   **b** jam   **c** stop

7 Most cities have a department ....
   a store   **b** market   **c** block

8 Maya lives in a house but I live in an apartment ....
   a park   **b** block   **c** stop

4 Complete the text with the words in the box.

> apartment block   bins   bus stop   car park
> department store   graffiti   park
> pedestrian crossing   rubbish   street lights

> I live on the 5th floor in an ¹............................. .
> At night you can see the ²............................. – and
> there are a lot! In front of my house, there's a
> ³............................. to get to the other side of the
> road. There's a ⁴............................. where you catch
> a bus to take you into town to the shops, like the
> new ⁵............................. that opened last week.
> It sells everything! Or you can drive and leave
> your car in the ⁶............................. . There's a
> ⁷............................. near my house too and a
> skateboard park with lots of ⁸.............................
> on the walls. But there isn't any ⁹.............................
> – people put it in the ¹⁰............................. . I like
> living in the town – we have everything!

READING

1 Read about these green cities. Write the topics mentioned in the correct column of the table. Sometimes more than one column is correct.

> animal life   cycles   parks   pollution   public transport   recycling   rubbish

Barcelona	Bogotá	Singapore	Adelaide

TALKING ABOUT ... GREEN CITIES AROUND THE WORLD

I chose Barcelona because I think it's a green city. There are lots of buses here and people often walk or ride their bike to school or walk. There is also a metro system and cable cars. I think that the pollution from transport is a really big problem, so Barcelona is a green city because it encourages people to take other forms of transport instead of their cars. But you have to pay and I don't think people should pay for transport.
Calen

Bogotá in Colombia is an interesting city because in 2014 they had a week where no cars were allowed into the city. There were buses but not many taxis. But for over thirty years they've had 'Cycle Sunday'. The roads become cycle paths. I think that's really cool because then you really think about the environment. The idea is that there is less pollution and everyone has to get into town in a 'green' way– walking, cycling, or bus.
Poppy

Singapore is a green city in Asia. Even the airport is green because there are gardens and a butterfly farm. That's so smart! In the past, there was a lot of pollution but now Singapore wants to be famous for being green. I found a website about green things in Singapore and things you can do. You can pick up the rubbish in your area with your friends. I think it's great and people learn that it's not good to drop rubbish.
Winston

I didn't think Australia had a lot of pollution but it does. Adelaide in South Australia is a green city. There are 29 parks and there's a big hotel there which recycles its energy and water. Also there are a lot of cycle paths and you can hire a bike for free. That's really good. There is a bus that doesn't use petrol: it is solar powered – you know, it uses energy from the sun! That's awesome!
Kelly

2 Read the text again. Which writer mentions the following?

1 a metro system   ....
2 buses that don't use petrol   ....
3 an area for insects in an airport   ....
4 a green hotel   ....
5 a day when you cannot use a car   ....
6 information about projects for young people   ....

3 Which writer …

1 was surprised by some information?   ....
2 thinks that the transport should not cost any money?   ....
3 thinks an idea is intelligent?   ....
4 likes an idea because it makes people think about the environment?   ....
5 thinks people need to learn to be tidy?   ....
6 thinks it's a good idea to reuse things?   ....

EP Word profile *light*

Match the questions and answers.

1 It's very dark in this room, isn't it?   ....   a No, but there's a light over there – switch it on!
2 Do you prefer winter or summer?   ....   b Nothing much – just something light.
3 Are you taking an umbrella?   ....   c I'm trying to light this match.
4 What are you doing?   ....   d Yes, there isn't any light from the sun.
5 What do you want for lunch?   ....   e No, it's only light rain.
6 Can you see anything?   ....   f Summer – I love the light evenings.

GRAMMAR *some/any, much/many, a lot of, a few/a little*

1 Complete the sentences with *some* or *any*.

1 She received .... beautiful flowers in hospital.

2 Have you got .... money?

3 You don't have to pay for .... of the buses.

4 There are .... places I really don't want to visit.

2 Complete the sentences with *much* or *many*.

1 I haven't got .... time – what do you want?

2 Felix didn't buy .... biscuits.

3 Did that phone cost .... ?

4 It's my first day – I don't know .... people.

3 Complete the sentences with *a little* or *a few*.

1 Help yourself to .... pieces of paper.

2 There's .... cake left – would you like it?

3 I just want .... information about the town, please.

4 Wait here – there are .... things I need to get from the shop.

4 Choose the correct word.

1 There's a boy in our class who eats .... chocolate.
 a a lot of   **b** many   **c** a few

2 I need to spend .... time thinking about this exercise.
 a any   **b** a few   **c** some

3 Jessie never has .... money. It's really annoying.
 a many   **b** a little   **c** any

4 There are .... interesting things to do in this town.
 a any   **b** many   **c** much

5 There are .... people here who don't use the internet regularly.
 a a few   **b** little   **c** any

6 There isn't .... we can do now – just wait for the party to begin!
 a many   **b** a little   **c** much

7 I can speak .... German.
 a a few   **b** a little   **c** much

8 Pablo moved to my school last week and he doesn't have .... friends yet.
 a many   **b** much   **c** some

9 Would you like .... coffee?
 a a few   **b** some   **c** much

10 I've nearly finished my homework – I just have .... questions to answer.
 a a little   **b** any   **c** a few

5 Read the text and choose the correct word.

The Whitsunday Islands are a group of islands in the middle of the Great Barrier Reef. [1] *Many / Much* of them don't have [2] *any / some* facilities, so you can't stay there, but there are [3] *some / a little* that have [4] *a few / a little* hotels. [5] *Much / A lot of* Australians like to spend their holidays on these islands because they are beautiful. If you need to relax, they are perfect because there isn't [6] *much / many* to do except swim in the beautiful blue sea. So all you need is [7] *a few / a little* time to book your next holiday in Paradise!

6 Complete the sentences with the words in the box.

> some   any   much   many
> a lot of   a few   a little

It's Cycle Day in Newtown and there are
[1]............................. bicycles for hire. Today's the day to go for a bike ride so there aren't [2].............................
people walking, and although we can see
[3]............................. tables at the café, they are empty.
We can see [4]............................. flags in the picture.
There's a wall with [5]............................. graffiti on it but not [6]............................. . There aren't [7].............................
animals in the picture.

7 ⊙ Choose the correct sentence in each pair.

1 **a** On my first day at a new school, I didn't have friends.
 b On my first day at a new school, I didn't have any friends.

2 **a** I went to the beach and I had a lot of fun.
 b I went to the beach and I had much fun.

3 **a** We can have lunch in a tent near the lake.
 b We can have lunch in some tent near the lake.

4 **a** Few hours later, they had to go back.
 b A few hours later, they had to go back.

5 **a** We do a lot of things together.
 b We do alot of things together.

VOCABULARY   Compounds: noun + noun

1 Add the missing vowels (A, E, I, O, U) to complete these words.

1 R........D   S....GN
2 P....ST   B....X
3 SP........D   L....M....T
4 T........R....ST   ....NF....RM....T........N
5 C....R   P....RK
6 R....CYCL....NG   B....N
7 B....S   ST....P
8 TH....   GR........ND   FL........R

2 Complete the sentences with the singular or plural form of a compound noun from exercise 1. Use each compound noun once.

1 Mum always parks in the same .... when we go into town.
2 The woman in the .... office can tell you about things happening in town.
3 .... in my country are yellow.
4 Look! The .... here is 20 km per hour. Slow down!
5 We live on ....
6 The number 65 stops at the .... opposite the cinema.
7 They empty our .... every other week.
8 There's a .... in Australia with a kangaroo on it.

LISTENING

1 Tick (✔) the things you can *clean up*.

1 bedroom ☐
2 river ☐
3 burgers ☐
4 desk ☐
5 computer ☐
6 house ☐
7 bag ☐
8 writing ☐

2 ▶4 Listen to a teacher introducing a class project. What are the students going to talk about?

1 how to clean their classroom
2 something they want to clean
3 interesting clean-up projects

3 ▶5 Now listen to the full conversation and complete the sentences with one word in each space.

1 Jenny talks about a project that is a .... for children on an Australian website.
2 Jenny chose a .... for a form of transport.
3 Jenny liked it because it teaches children about a .... in a fun way.
4 Greg's project is about cleaning up a .... in the USA.
5 Greg found it on the .... of an American history museum.

4 ▶6 Listen to another student, Meg, talking about her project. Complete the text with one word in each space.

Well, I actually took part in a 'clean-up [1] ....
beach' day. There was a big [2] .... of people and we all [3] .... at the bus stop in front of the beach. There was a man who [4] .... us what to do. We had big [5] .... bags and we collected any [6] .... that we found. We were in different [7] .... and we worked together. It was a really [8] .... day but it's a pity people [9] .... all this rubbish. It's easy to put it in the [10] .... !

5 ▶7 Listen to the conversations again. Are these sentences true (T) or false (F)?

1 Jenny talked about a game for adults. ......
2 You have to do something for the environment in the game. ......
3 Jenny learnt things by playing the game. ......
4 She thinks she and her friends should do something similar. ......
5 Greg visited the museum to help clean it up. ......
6 The teacher liked both Jenny and Greg's projects. ......
7 Meg's project was about cleaning up bus stops. ......

7 Getting on

VOCABULARY be, do, have and make

1 Choose the correct verb in each sentence.

1 It .... me angry when my sister goes into my bedroom.
   a makes **b** does **c** has

2 Vicki is .... problems with her maths homework – can you help?
   a making **b** doing **c** having

3 My brother and I .... an argument this evening about washing the dishes.
   a made **b** had **c** did

4 When you called yesterday, I .... on my own.
   a was **b** had **c** have

5 Do you want to .... something for Dad's birthday?
   a be **b** do **c** have

6 We always .... fun at Annie's house – she has a swimming pool!
   a have **b** make **c** are

7 Can you .... me a favour?
   a do **b** make **c** have

8 I .... lots of new friends at my new school.
   a did **b** made **c** was

9 John helped me with my homework when he .... here yesterday.
   a had **b** did **c** was

10 I really like Mary – we .... lots in common.
   a do **b** have **c** make

2 Match the questions and answers and add the correct form of the verb.

be	be	do	have	have	make

1 What's the matter with John? ....
2 Did you break this? ....
3 Do you get on with your cousin? ....
4 Is that Phil and his Dad over there? ....
5 Do you want to go for a run? ....
6 Are you OK? ....

a Not really, but we can .... something when you get back.
b Not really. We don't .... anything in common.
c Well sort of, but it .... my fault.
d Yes, but this TV show .... me really angry.
e No one knows but something .... wrong.
f Yes! They're .... an argument about the football!

3 Complete the text with the words and phrases in the box.

angry	argument	fault	friends	in common
on my own		something		wrong

This morning I woke up late. It wasn't my
¹ .... – the alarm clock didn't go off.
I got up quickly and wanted to go into the bathroom but my sister was there. She takes a long time every morning and it makes me ² ....
I knocked on the door, but there was no answer. Then we had an ³ .... because she said she only had a 3-minute shower. Right! – not! and she finally came out. I quickly had a shower and breakfast, and then caught the bus – just in time. I'm usually ⁴ .... on the bus because it's hard to make ⁵ .... – I don't think I have anything ⁶ .... with the people at my school. But at the next bus stop, a boy my age got on the bus and he looked like me – unhappy. I asked him if something was ⁷ .... 'My sister!' he replied. We started chatting and soon we planned to do ⁸ .... together after school. I'm glad I woke up late!

EP Word profile *like*

Write the words in the correct order and add *like*.

1 you / eating / sushi / Do?
....

2 is / Phil / brother / his / just
....

3 your / teacher / What's / new / ?
....

4 taking / rain / I'm / it / umbrella / looks / my / because
....

5 shopping centres / Dad / to / hates / places / going
....

6 me / dislikes / your / Tell / and / about
....

READING

1 Tick (✔) the sentences that you think are true.

1 All grandparents are older than you. ☐
2 Some grandparents do not understand younger people. ☐
3 Most grandparents have lots of stories to tell. ☐
4 All grandparents want to visit places. ☐

2 Read the first paragraph quickly. Tick (✔) what you think the article is going to be about.

1 interesting activities you do with your grandparents ☐
2 how you feel about your grandparents ☐
3 arguments with your grandparents ☐

3 Read the whole text and check your answers to exercise 2.

4 Read the text again. Are these sentences true (T) or false (F)?

1 All of the readers get on with their grandparents. ....
2 Giuliana's grandmother lives in a different town. ....
3 Giuliana shares an interest with her grandmother. ....
4 Giuliana's grandmother is teaching her something she already knows. ....
5 Andy's granddad is good at sports. ....
6 Andy and Boris' granddads make them laugh. ....
7 Boris' grandfather is a serious man. ....
8 Boris' grandparents don't visit as often as they did. ....

Grandparents = Grand people

Last month we asked you to send us your ideas about grandparents. We received some very interesting answers! Some of you describe your grandparents as friends. They are the people you talk to when you have to talk to an adult but you don't want to talk to your mum or dad. They help you, they're there for you and they don't disagree with you. But there are a few of you who have grandparents who live in different towns, or even abroad, and so you don't see them very often.

Grandparents are special people and we love ours! Here's what you say.

Giuliana Ross, Canada

I love everyone in my family but my grandma is really special for me. She lives a few streets away from us, so when I want to be on my own I usually walk to her house. She doesn't ask questions. I love that! We do lots of things together too like making food, which we love. At the moment, she's teaching me to make her favourite dish that her grandmother taught her. It's quite hard to do but I love sharing moments with her. It's special.

Andy Davidson, USA

I love my granddad! He's just the best – he can keep a secret, he helps me and he's really funny! We have lots of fun and we have lots in common. We both enjoy going climbing! My granddad is really good at that – no one realises that he's in his sixties!

Boris Sanneh, UK

My grandparents live in another country. They visit us about every three years but it's hard because we don't really know what to talk about. They ask about school and stuff. That's usually the first week. By the second week though, things are a bit better and it's more 'natural'. When my sister and I were younger, they visited more often and I remember Grandpa doing silly things like making faces when Mum wasn't looking. He still does that sometimes. But now that they are elderly, I'd like them to live closer.

Next week:

Older brothers and sisters – do you get on well?

Write in with your experiences to portia@yourteenmag.com.

5 Match the highlighted words in the text to their meanings.

1 small and not important ....
2 old ....
3 in or to a foreign country ....
4 something you tell no one or only a few people ....
5 notices or understands something ....
6 food prepared as part of a meal ....

6 Complete the sentences with the correct form of the words from exercise 5.

1 This .... smells delicious! Yum!
2 Stop being .... ! It's not funny.
3 .... people sometimes find it hard to stay awake.
4 Can you keep a .... ?
5 Alex and his family always go .... in the summer.
6 They didn't .... the train was at midday.

GRAMMAR *have to, must, should*

1 **Write the words in the correct order to make sentences.**

1 has / practise / piano / to / the / Zoe / every day

....

2 library / be / You / must / in / quiet / the

....

3 mustn't / in / room / run / dining / the / You

....

4 had / to / Grandma / 5 km / cycle / school / to

....

5 don't / We / to / have / tomorrow / school / to / go

....

6 lunch / to / my / I / make / had / own / yesterday

....

2 **Choose the best answer in each sentence.**

1 Johnny left basketball early last week – he .... do his homework.
   a had to   b must   c didn't have to

2 Can you keep a secret? You .... tell anyone!
   a don't have to   b must   c mustn't

3 When the film starts, you .... be quiet.
   a don't have to   b had to   c must

4 Mum .... wear glasses to read – she can't see properly without them.
   a must   b has to   c didn't have to

5 I think you .... tell us what happened.
   a should   b didn't have to   c mustn't

6 Mike and Tracey .... get up early tomorrow – it's the holidays!
   a don't have to   b doesn't have to   c mustn't

7 Thank you! That's a lovely present but you .... get me anything!
   a don't have to   b didn't have to   c mustn't

8 You .... argue so much! It's isn't good.
   a must   b have to   c shouldn't

9 You .... be late for school or the teacher will be really angry.
   a don't have to   b mustn't   c should

10 I wasn't sure what to write for my school project so I asked Dad what I .... do.
   a should   b had to   c must

3 **Complete the text with the verbs in the box.**

> didn't have to   don't have to   had to
> have to   should   shouldn't

My brother Martin and I share a bedroom. He's a bit messy and so I often ¹............................ tidy up his side of the bedroom. I know I ²............................ really, but I don't like it when there are things all over the floor. Mum thinks we argue and says I ³............................ go into his side of the room but my brother doesn't mind. Sometimes he says, 'You ⁴............................ clean up faster!' But it's a joke! Grandpa told me that he ⁵............................ share a bedroom with one brother – he ⁶............................ share a bedroom with four! I can't imagine that!

SORRY KIDS, YOU HAVE TO WEAR YOUR SCHOOL UNIFORMS.

4 **Complete the sentences with *should* or *shouldn't*.**

1 You .... go to bed early when you have school the next day.

2 You .... eat a lot of fast food – it's bad for you.

3 You .... find someone to ask about your homework.

4 Erik .... behave in class – it's annoying for everyone when he doesn't.

5 I .... really play these computer games – they are a waste of time!

6 We .... make a reservation at the restaurant for your birthday dinner.

5 👁 **Correct the mistakes in these sentences or tick (✔) any you think are correct.**

1 You will bring a ball if you want to play football.

....

....

2 I have to prepare for the picnic.

....

....

3 It must be fun if we go together.

....

....

4 The rules of this game are that you should help the monkey to find her home.

....

....

5 So you must to believe me, this game is the best.

....

....

VOCABULARY Phrasal verbs: friendships

1 Write the letters in the correct order to make phrasal verbs.

1 TOGHANU ....

2 ETGIWNOHT ....

3 TOGTEETHERG ....

4 ATULFOL ....

2 Complete the text message using the correct form of the verbs from exercise 1.

Hi James! I'm glad you are ¹ .... your new friend, Philippe. Gina says he's great at tennis! Have you heard about Gina and François? They ² .... last week but I think they're friends again now. Let's ³ .... on Saturday for a game and then we can ⁴ .... with everyone else in town. I think we should invite François and Gina too! What do you think? Text me back today! ☺

WRITING Rules for friendship

1 Read the text below. Which topic is Sabrina writing about?

1 Your best friend

2 A person you admire

3 A friend in a different class

My best friend is called Max. We're the same age and we get on really well. We love the same things and we have a lot of fun together. He usually comes to my house at the weekend and we play games on the computer. My parents like him too and he always remembers my mum's birthday! Sometimes we don't have to say anything because we know what the other person is thinking! We never fall out – it's great! I think friends are really important because they often understand you better than your parents. He's like a brother – he's my best mate!

By Sabrina

2 Find words and phrases in Sabrina's text that mean:

1 a friend ....

2 enjoy doing things together ....

3 to have a good relationship ....

4 to have arguments with someone and stop being friendly ....

3 Read the text again and put these ideas in order. Write the numbers 1–4.

a something special about your friend ☐

b personal information about your best friend ☐

c things you can do together ☐

d why friends are important ☐

4 Read these ideas. Tick (✔) the ones that you think are important. Add some of your own.

• Be honest. ☐

• Listen to your friend when he/she has a problem. ☐

• Laugh at them all the time. ☐

• Don't have arguments – real friends don't argue. ☐

• Hang out with each other all the time. ☐

• Do things together and on your own. ☐

....

....

Friends are great but BEST FRIENDS are the BEST!

But how do you keep your best friend?

What do you do if you have an argument?

What advice can you give?

Send me your top three rules for friends by next Tuesday. rosalindworthington@yourfaveteenmag.com

5 Read the magazine ad. Write your three rules for friends.

• Write about 80–100 words.

• Remember to check your spelling and grammar.

8 Going away

VOCABULARY Travel

1 Match the words in the box to their meanings.

> backpack   check-in desk   customs   passport   queue   sign   ticket

1 a line of people waiting for something, one behind the other   ....
2 the place at an airport where you go to say you have arrived for your flight   ....
3 a document, often a book, that you need to enter or leave a country   ....
4 a bag that you carry on your back   ....
5 a small piece of paper that shows you have paid to do something.   ....
6 the place where your bags are examined when you are going into a country   ....
7 a notice in a public place which gives information or instructions   ....

2 Match the words from 1–5 with a–e to make compound nouns.

1 departure   ....   **a** check
2 passport   ....   **b** hall
3 security   ....   **c** gate
4 boarding   ....   **d** control
5 baggage   ....   **e** pass

3 Choose the correct answer in each sentence.

1 You usually show your .... pass as you get onto the plane.
   a security   **b** boarding   **c** departure
2 Your bags are sometimes checked at the .... control.
   a passport   **b** check-in   **c** gate
3 If you don't know where to go in an airport look at a ....
   a ticket   **b** passport   **c** sign
4 It's a good idea to get to an airport early because there are often long ....
   a queues   **b** tickets   **c** customs
5 If you are going to a different country, you need a ....
   a sign   **b** passport   **c** backpack
6 The last place before you get on the plane is the .... gate.
   a departure   **b** check-in   **c** customs

4 Complete the text with words from exercises 1 and 2.

So, I'm ready to go and I know what to do! I printed my [1]........................... last night and today I added a few things to my [2]........................... . It weighs exactly 23 kg – I hope it'll be OK when I get to the [3]........................... .
Tomorrow we're getting up at 6 am – Dad's going to drive me to the airport. I have to follow the [4]........................... to check in for Paris. Then I'll go through [5]........................... and show my [6]........................... and through the [7]........................... . I really hope there isn't a [8]........................... because I want to get to the [9]........................... quickly. Then I fly to Paris! When I get to Paris I'll go through [10]........................... , then get my bag from the [11]........................... and meet up with my cousin, Stefano. He's got the [12]........................... for the train to Marseilles! I'm excited ... and scared!

READING

1 Look at the text in each question. What does it say?

1

> Keep your boarding pass beyond the departure gate to show to cabin staff.

A Passengers must have boarding passes ready for checking on the plane.
B Check-in staff can advise travellers of any change to their departure gate.
C Staff at this departure gate will collect all boarding passes as you leave.

2

> *To avoid feeling sick at sea, take tablets with water 30 minutes before sailing.*

A Wait at least 30 minutes before taking more of these tablets.
B You need to take these tablets in advance of your departure.
C If you are feeling sick on board, have these tablets with water.

2 Read the article quickly. Tick (✔) the best title.

1 How to close your suitcase ☐
2 Going on holiday? What to take and how to take it ☐
3 What <u>not</u> to pack for a holiday ☐

3 Read the article again. Choose the correct answer.

1 The person who wrote the article is ....
   a a professional writer
   b a reader

2 The author says strong bags are a good idea because ....
   a they travel better
   b they are often larger

3 When thinking about the clothes to take, generally she suggests taking ....
   a more than you think you need
   b less than you think you need

4 The article tells you that when you pack for a summer holiday, ...
   a you need two swimsuits
   b make sure you have enough shoes

5 Having lots of bags means ....
   a you can easily find what you're looking for
   b you can pack more quickly

6 Writing about your holiday is a good idea ....
   a so you don't get bored
   b so you don't forget what you did

7 The author says it's a good idea to ....
   a think about what to take just before you go
   b check that everything will go into your bag

4 Complete the sentences with the highlighted words from the text.

1 Our .... to New York was cancelled because the weather was bad.
2 Florida is a popular holiday ....
3 You could see the fish swimming because the water was so ....
4 Can you give me some .... about what to pack when we visit you next month?
5 Julie wrote in her .... every day on holiday.
6 The .... to the problem was not easy.

EP Word profile around

Add around in the correct place in these sentences.

1 We walked the airport but we couldn't find a bookshop.
2 I'm not sure of Kevin's address, but he definitely lives somewhere here.
3 If you're travelling the countryside, remember to take plenty of water.
4 My brother last visited Argentina four years ago.
5 Wendy stopped on the stairs above me and looked.
6 There were sixteen of us, all sitting the campfire to keep warm.

You wrote it!

So, you're going on a summer holiday and your mum says you have to pack your bag yourself! What now? Here are some tips for packing that I've learnt the hard way!

○ First, find out how much you can take – if you are going on a long flight, you can sometimes take more, but not always, so it's important to check. Make sure your bag is a strong one of good quality. Once, when I went to get my bag, I realised that it was open! Everyone could see what was in my bag! Oops!

○ Find out what you're going to do and what the weather will be like at your destination. Then make a list of all the clothes you plan to take. And then divide that in half, so if you have four tops, take two. One year, I went on holiday and I didn't wear half the clothes I had with me! So ask yourself a few questions like do you really need five pairs of shoes? (No!) Also, if it's a summer holiday, you're probably going to be wearing your swimsuit most of the time. Make sure you pack two – nothing worse than trying to get into a wet swimsuit!

○ Do you hate that feeling when you can't find what you're looking for in your bag? Me too! Placing smaller bags inside the bigger bag is the best solution. That way you can easily reach everything.

○ It's essential to take things to keep yourself busy while you're travelling and while you're relaxing by the pool. Don't leave it too late to think about your holiday reading and listening. Create some holiday playlists for your phone and find some new books by your favourite authors. You could also keep a diary so that in the cold winter months you can read about your wonderful summer! Also if you're travelling by plane, don't forget that any liquids have to be in a clear plastic bag.

○ Don't leave packing until the last moment. Make a list of everything you need about two weeks before. Then get everything ready. You can also pop it into your bag a couple of days before – just check it all fits!

GRAMMAR Future: *be going to* and present continuous

1 Write the words in the correct order to make sentences.

1 going / to / next year / visit / Paris / We're

....

2 clean / to / it's / her / car / going / because / dirty / Mum's

....

3 are / My / without / holiday / parents / a / Bali / having / in / me / !

....

4 homework / to / I'm / do / going / my / now

....

5 is / Tom / buy / going / a / to / phone / new

....

6 basketball / are / playing / for / the / team / James and Noah / school

....

7 going / our tickets / Zac and I / for / are / the music festival / to buy

....

8 there / It / to / isn't / aren't / rain / because / any rain clouds / going

....

2 Complete the conversation with the present continuous or *going to* form of the verbs in the box.

do   fill in   go   have   return   take

Lily: Hey Tyler what ¹............................ later?

Tyler: I ²............................ that form for the summer camp.

Lily: Oh really? ³............................ camping this year? I didn't think you wanted to go.

Tyler: Yeah, I know, but it was fun last year. And I think they ⁴............................ different sports, like rock climbing. Also, everyone from last year's camp ⁵............................ . I can't wait to see Stacie and Jonas!

Lily: Well, I think it sounds great – but I can't go. Mum and Dad ⁶............................ me to an adventure park in the USA this summer.

Tyler: Lucky you!

3 Read the sentences and choose the correct verb.

1 Emilia is *going to visit / visiting* her aunt this afternoon.

2 The Maz family are *flying / going to fly* to the Caribbean for their summer holiday on Monday.

3 I think I'm *going to watch / watching* TV tonight. I don't want to go out.

4 We're *leaving / going to leave* at 5 am tomorrow – don't be late!

5 We're *going to buy / buying* new bikes soon.

6 Look out! That car isn't *going to stop / stopping*.

7 We're *studying / going to study* animals in biology next week.

8 Marcia is *going to be / being* late to school again.

4 ⊙ Choose the correct sentence in each pair.

1 a Tomorrow we are going to the beach.
  b Tomorrow we go to the beach.

2 a I think that you going to like this game a lot.
  b I think that you are going to like this game a lot.

3 a We are excited because next week we have a party!
  b We are excited because next week we are having a party!

4 a On Saturday we are going to have a picnic.
  b On Saturday we have a picnic.

5 a Next Saturday my family and I are going to a picnic.
  b Next Saturday my family and I going to a picnic.

VOCABULARY Phrasal verbs: travel

1 Make phrasal verbs with a word from box A and a word from box B to match the definitions.

A | check   get   go   set   take |

B | away   back   in   off   off |

1 leave your home in order to spend time in a different place ....

2 start a journey ....

3 return to a place after you have been somewhere else ....

4 leave the ground and fly on a plane ....

5 say who you are when you arrive at a hotel and get the key ....

2 Complete the conversation with the correct form of the phrasal verbs from exercise 1. Add any other words you need.

A: So when ¹............................ ?

B: On Monday. We ²............................ at 5 am, I think.

A: Really? Why are you leaving so early?

B: Well, we have to ³............................ and get to the departure gate.

A: Sure, but what time does the plane ⁴............................ ?

B: At 8.30 am.

A: Ah, OK. And when ⁵............................ ?

B: In two weeks' time! It's going to be brilliant!

LISTENING

1 ▶8 **Listen to Aymer and Jane. What are they talking about?**

1 special holiday destinations
2 people and journeys
3 places they want to go on holiday

2 ▶8 **Listen again. Are these sentences true (T) or false (F)?**

1 Aymer is going to talk about the first people who went to the Antarctic. ....
2 Aymer says he understands how making long and difficult journeys changed people. ....
3 The teens comment on how the early explorers didn't have the technology they have today. ....
4 Jane is going to talk about someone who travelled with other people. ....
5 Jane understands why people might make these journeys. ....
6 Aymer says he doesn't want to go on a journey like that yet. ....

3 ▶8 **Listen again. Complete the sentences with the words in the box.**

> Antarctic   Canada   horses
> journeys   mobile phones

1 Aymer is going to write about people who went to the ....
2 Jane's topic is about a journey across ....
3 Her explorer took .... with her.
4 Neither explorer had ....
5 The teens are excited about the .... they are going to talk about.

4 ▶9 **Listen to part of the conversation again and complete the sentences.**

> I think I'll have to [1]............................ about how their lives changed. But that was an [2]............................ journey – especially as they didn't have the [3]............................ we have [4]............................ !

5 **Match the words from the conversation to their meanings.**

1 equipment   ....
2 guess   ....
3 explore   ....
4 experience   ....
5 incredible   ....
6 nowadays   ....

a in the present time, not in the past
b the things you need for a particular purpose
c very good or exciting
d when you try to think of the answer to something that you don't know
e something that happens to you that affects how you feel
f to go around a place where you have never been in order to find out what is there

9 Shop till you drop

VOCABULARY Money and shopping

1 Complete the crossword using the clues below.

Across

2 you get this back if you pay more for something than it costs

8 the amount of money that you pay to buy something

9 the place in a shop where you pay for your goods

Down

1 keep money so that you can buy something with it in the future (two words)

3 a price which is lower than usual (two words)

4 to return something to the place you bought it from (two words)

5 you keep your money in this and take it out when you need to (two words)

6 a piece of paper that proves that you have received goods or money

7 give something to someone without asking for payment (two words)

2 Choose the correct words to complete the sentences.

1 My friend is *saving up / taking back* to buy a new phone.

2 I opened a *checkout / bank account* last week to put my money in.

3 Let's go to that new clothes shop – there are lots of *special offers / receipts*.

4 I can't return this broken CD – I've lost the *price / receipt*.

5 The *change / price* of clothes online is often cheaper than in a shop.

6 This doesn't fit – I'll *take it back / save it up* tomorrow.

7 Helene has got a part-time job at the *checkout / receipt* in our local supermarket.

8 I always *take back / give away* my old clothes to second-hand shops.

9 I gave you £5.00, so I need £2.00 *change / price* please.

3 Complete the conversation with the correct form of the words from exercise 1.

Juliet: Look at this beautiful new pair of trainers. Oh, and this shop has them on
¹............................. .

Will: Yeah – that's a really good ²............................. for those trainers. Let's go!

In the shop

Juliet: There they are! OK, cool – with my birthday money I'm sure I have enough ³............................. , but I'll just check my ⁴............................. with the app on my phone. Yep! Cool!

Will: OK, well, here's the ⁵............................. , time to pay!

(gives money)

Shop assistant: Thank you. Oh wait! That's too much. Here's your ⁶............................. and your ⁷............................. . Have a nice day!

Will: Thank you! Don't lose that Juliet, if you have to ⁸............................. them .... , you must have it.

Juliet: Not necessary! They're perfect! Look!

Will: Hope so! If not, you will have to ⁹............................. them ....!

READING

1 Read the first paragraph quickly. What do you think 'second-hand' means?

1 You can't buy them.
2 Someone else owned or used them first.
3 They are not for sale – you can only borrow them.

2 Read the whole text and complete the sentences with one or two words in each space.

1 Some second-hand shops give their money to ....
2 Many teens find interesting .... in these shops.
3 Second-hand shopping in Australia is called ....
4 Elise and her friends have to find special clothes for the ....
5 Mark's dad used to collect things at country ....
6 Mark recently found a .... in a second-hand shop.
7 Mark enjoys the .... for cheap things.
8 Liane writes about a .... that is now a shop.

3 Match the highlighted words in the text to their meanings.

1 broken in some way so that it doesn't work properly ....
2 liked by many people ....
3 describes someone who has original and unusual ideas ....
4 a group that gives money, food, or help to people who need it ....
5 we use this word for a lot of different things together when we can't say exactly what they are ....
6 get and keep things of one type such as stamps or coins as a hobby ....
7 when you try to find something ....

EP Word profile *change*

Complete the sentences with a suitable form of *change*.

1 I've .... the book you gave me for another one – I hope that's OK!
2 Mum and I bought all this food in the market, which was a real .... from shopping in the supermarket.
3 My aunt hates .... trains when she comes to visit us.
4 Are there any .... to tomorrow's timetable?
5 That café we like has .... its opening hours again!
6 Haven't you given me too much .... ? These biscuits cost 95 pence.
7 I went home and .... into a smart shirt and trousers for the school concert.
8 We mustn't forget about .... our money into pounds before we leave.

SECOND-HAND SHOPPING

Second-hand shopping is big in some countries like the UK and Australia. When people get tired of their clothes, or they have too many things, they sometimes give them to second-hand shops. Second-hand charity shops use the money from the goods they sell to help people who are ill or have problems. And recently these shops have become very popular with teens because you can find different, fun, cheap items! This is what three second-hand shoppers said.

Here in Australia we call it 'op shopping' – that's opportunity shopping, so you find something and you're like 'wow! This is so cool and it's so cheap!' My friends and I love op shopping, and we go quite a lot. But the main time for us to do it is when we have a school festival. We have to find crazy clothes of one colour – last year it was yellow! That's when op shops are great!
Elise Fieldstone, Perth, Australia

My Dad used to go to country markets looking for items to collect and I remember once when I was about 9 years old, he gave me £5.00 and told me to buy whatever I wanted. It was great. I got a whole Lego set and a toy train. I was keen on second-hand stuff from that day! Last week I bought a really cool 1980s leather jacket for not much at all! You have to look carefully and there are things that you don't want, you know, because they're old or damaged. But the fun is in the search!
Mark McCarthy, Manchester, UK

My favourite hobby is reading. I just love it. And so all the second-hand bookshops are just wonderful for me! I spend hours in them! A few months ago a new second-hand bookshop opened in my town. It's interesting because it's actually a house, and the owner has put all the cookbooks in the kitchen – how creative is that!! It's great because you see books that you didn't know about and also you can discover old books – and as they are second-hand, the price is right!
Liane Patel, Auckland, New Zealand

GRAMMAR Present perfect, questions and short answers

1 Write the past participle of these irregular verbs.

1 become ....
2 find ....
3 give ....
4 sell ....
5 buy ....
6 spend ....
7 take ....
8 go ....

2 Write full sentences from these words, using the present perfect.

1 I / write / a letter / the newspaper
....

2 Jayde / take / beautiful photos / with an old camera
....

3 Alda / eat / all the chocolate!
....

4 Jan / never / read / an online newspaper
....

5 Louise / catch / a bad cold
....

6 you / ever / buy / shoes / from a second-hand shop?
....

3 Complete the text with the correct form of the verbs in brackets.

> Hi Mollie!
> You wanted to know something about me. Well, I ¹ .... (never / visit) the UK – but maybe one day I will! I've
> ² .... (never / swim) in the sea either, because there is no sea in Switzerland, but I ³ .... (be) in the lake plenty of times. I've ⁴ .... (never / eat) raw fish, you know, sushi, but I
> ⁵ .... (drink) white hot chocolate – that's delicious! What about you – what things
> ⁶ .... (you / do)?
> Write soon,
> Rick

4 Match the questions and answers.

1 Do you know Jack? ....
2 Has your mum ever given you a present that you didn't like? ....
3 Have you ever been on your own for a long time? ....
4 Have you ever bought something without telling your parents? ....
5 Have you ever received too little change in a shop? ....
6 Have you ever been to a foreign country? ....

a No, she knows what I like!
b No, I haven't – they know everything I buy!
c Yes, once, but then the woman gave me the right money.
d No, I've never met him.
e No, but I want to visit Canada.
f No, I like being with other people!

5 ⊙ Correct the mistakes in these sentences or tick (✔) any you think are correct.

1 You have heard about it or not?
....

2 Have you ever have an argument?
....

3 Today, I am very happy as I have received my new computer game.
....

4 I know her all my life.
....

5 Did you ever play a game named Heroes of Newerth?
....

VOCABULARY *been* and *gone*

1 Choose the correct answer.

1 Jake isn't here. He's *been* / *gone* home.
2 Where's Maggie? Has she *been* / *gone* to the library for the book club?
3 I haven't *been* / *gone* to your house.
4 We've *been* / *gone* to London many times.
5 Terese isn't here. She's *been* / *gone* to the shops.
6 Have you *been* / *gone* to the new sports club? It's amazing.

2 Complete the messages with either *been* or *gone*.

> I've ¹ .... to the gym. Back at 7 pm.

> If you're reading this, you've ² .... to the doctor's and you're back! Call them – you left your bag there!

> James has ³ .... to the library for you and collected your books. They're here.

> Pip,
> We've ⁴ .... to visit Grandma – back later. Mum

WRITING   A blog entry

See Prepare to write box, Student's Book page 35.

1 **Where do you write down your thoughts? Tick (✔) any that you use.**

- in a notebook that I write in by hand ☐
- on my phone ☐
- on my blog ☐
- I don't write but I take photos and put them on my Instagram ☐
- I don't – they're in my head ☐

2 **Read Winnie's blog. What is she writing about?**

> Posted @ 2.14 pm
>
> Hi guys!
>
> It's my birthday tomorrow and I'm really excited. I'm not sure what Mum and Dad are giving me but I've asked for lots of things. Angie, my sister, is fairly sure that they've bought me a new computer. That would be very good as I need one for school – and playing games of course!
>
> I don't know what Angie is going to give me. She's told me it's big but I think she's joking!
>
> It doesn't matter what I get – I know I will like everything! Also I think Mum has invited our cousins for a surprise dinner! They're a bit silly but it'll be a great evening!
>
> Winnie

3 **Look at these words from exercise 2. Do they make the adjectives stronger (S) or weaker (W)?**

1 really ....
2 fairly ....
3 very ....
4 a bit ....

4 **Choose the correct answer.**

1 I can't wait until tomorrow – it's going to be *really / a bit* wonderful.
2 Irene is *a bit / very* shy and doesn't always like speaking in front of the class.
3 Dad's wearing shorts today! But it is *very / fairly* warm I guess!
4 I'm going to bed now – I'm *fairly / really* tired.
5 I'm *fairly / really* confident that I've passed my exam, but you can never be sure.
6 The lady in that shop is *really / a bit* helpful – she always helps me find what I want.

5 **Write an entry for your blog. Read the situation.**

> It's the first day of a new school term tomorrow.
> How do you feel?
> Have you bought everything you need?
> Which friends do you want to see?

- Write your diary entry.
- Write about 80–100 words.
- Remember to check your spelling and grammar.

VOCABULARY   Food and drink adjectives

1 Find twelve food words in the word square (→ ↓).

L	V	R	D	R	A	W	J	K	M	Y
J	D	F	E	R	N	D	H	T	Q	R
W	I	M	L	Q	W	Y	O	S	Q	W
Z	S	B	I	T	T	E	R	O	T	Y
N	G	J	C	P	S	T	R	U	H	R
S	U	N	I	G	W	A	I	R	X	M
P	S	Z	O	T	E	S	B	M	F	G
I	T	L	U	T	E	T	L	N	R	Y
C	I	K	S	C	T	Y	E	Y	E	X
Y	N	Y	K	J	U	I	C	Y	S	B
R	G	F	R	O	Z	E	N	K	H	C

2 Write the words from the word square next to their meanings.

1 full of juice ....
2 with a good flavour and nice to eat ....
3 with a taste like sugar ....
4 produced or collected recently ....
5 with a taste or smell like a lemon ....
6 having a very pleasant taste or smell ....
7 a strong taste that is not sweet ....
8 containing ingredients with a strong, hot flavour ....
9 unpleasant or bad ....
10 made cold and hard to keep for a long time ....
11 extremely unpleasant ....
12 not cooked ....

3 Choose the correct adjective.

1 Carol likes eating curries that are hot and *bitter / spicy*.
2 Andy and Brad bought some *frozen / fresh* vegetables from the market.
3 Yum! This is really *tasty / raw*. What is it ?
4 Dad made dinner again it's really *horrible / juicy* – he can't cook!
5 This pineapple is really *sweet / frozen*. It's come from Barbados.
6 Mum can eat a whole lemon! I don't know how she does it – it's so *sour / delicious*.
7 Would you like some peaches? They are really *juicy / bitter*.
8 I don't think this fish is cooked enough – it's still *raw / sweet* in the middle.

> **EP Word profile** *really*
>
> Add (*not*) *really* to these sentences in the correct place.
>
> 1 Are you warm enough? No, not.
> 2 Jared didn't do that homework himself.
> 3 That film was great.
> 4 Ben shouldn't go out today – it's too cold.
> 5 **A:** So then our teacher told us to go home.
>   **B:** Lucky you!

READING

1 Which of the following fruits come the hottest parts of the world? Which are from cooler parts?

| apple | banana | pear | pineapple | mango | strawberry |

Hotter	Cooler

2 Read Marta's blog and put the events in order. Write the numbers 1–6.

a Her parents decided to visit a farm. ☐
b Marta wrote her blog post. ☐
c Her parents' friends arrived from another country. ☐
d They went on a tour of the farm. ☐
e Marta took her school books with her. ☐
f A man offered Marta a piece of strange fruit. ☐

Hi guys! Just wanted to tell you what I've done recently. Well, we had some visitors from the UK and so Mum and Dad thought it would be nice to take them to Tropical Fruit World. They said, 'We haven't been, so let's go together. It looks interesting.' I know – it sounds so dull! I don't know how anyone could think it's interesting to go to a fruit farm! Anyhow, I had to go so I took my music and books for some school work and planned to have a drink in the café.

We got there and there weren't many people and there were all these strange-looking fruits. A man asked me if I wanted to try some chocolate pudding fruit! I was like, 'What is that!?' I tried it and it really tasted like chocolate pudding. Then we tried others including jackfruit, which tastes like pineapple and banana together, and dragon fruit, which has a sweet taste. It's a bit odd but really delicious. There's also a chewing gum fruit, star apples and many more! It was so interesting – I had no idea.

Then we went on a walk with a woman from the farm, Betty. She showed us fifty different kinds of mango! I honestly thought there was just one variety of mango! Not true! Betty told us about many other amazing fruits too. Finally, we went to the café and tried some of them. In the end, I have to say it was a real adventure and I was really pleased I went!

#fruit #thanks #mumanddad #parentsknowbest

3 Complete the sentences with the highlighted words from the text.

1 You can sometimes find .... fruits in the supermarket.
2 This book is really .... – nothing is happening in it.
3 Mum usually makes a .... for Sunday lunch.
4 You can buy a .... of teas as a present for Grandma.
5 Look at this .... message I've received. Do you understand it?

4 Read Marta's entry again and choose the correct answer.

1 Marta visited the fruit farm *with her parents / on her own*.
2 Marta planned to *do her homework / sit in the car* while her parents were visiting the fruit farm.
3 When they arrived at the farm, they tried some fruits *they didn't know / that were familiar to them*.
4 Marta thought all the new fruit was *disgusting / tasty*.
5 Before Marta went to the farm, she *knew / didn't realise* that there were so many different mangoes.
6 By the end of her blog entry Marta is *positive / disappointed* about the fruit farm.

GRAMMAR Present perfect and past simple, *How long?* and *for/since*

1 Complete the sentences with the correct form of the verbs in brackets.

1 Frank .... here since he was five years old. (live)

2 I .... sushi many times. (eat)

3 Mum .... an amazing meal for my birthday last week. (prepare)

4 Anja .... me to her party night last week. (not invite)

5 My Mum .... that mountain many times – she loves seeing the view from the top! (climb)

6 Perry and Max .... on a camel before. (ride)

7 Uncle Tim .... by plane before so he's a bit nervous. (not travel)

8 I .... about this for a long time. (not write)

9 Mum and Dad .... with Auntie Betty when they were in London last week. (stay)

10 You .... this exercise – well done! (finish)

2 Write full sentences from these words, using the present perfect or past simple.

1 Chris / often / eat / food / from / Malaysia

....

2 Marcia / attend / music festival / last year

....

3 That team / not score / a goal / for a long time

....

4 Bobby / not call / me / yesterday

....

5 you / visit / castle / on / holiday / last year?

....

6 In / end / the family / not keep / the little cat

....

7 John / not send / you / text / for / ages

....

8 Dave / live / New Zealand / for / three years / loves it

....

9 Mum and Dad / get married / a long time / ago

....

10 Jake / collect / his parcel / from / post office / today

....

3 Complete the sentences with *for* or *since*.

1 That shop has been there .... about three months now.

2 Christine has played tennis .... she was seven years old.

3 Pete has known his best friend, Joe, ... he joined the club.

4 I've had this jumper .... ages. It's my favourite.

5 The boys have been waiting here .... twenty minutes.

6 I haven't read a book .... last holidays.

7 I've known my best friend .... five years.

8 We haven't seen Billy .... last April.

9 My Aunt has been in India .... three months.

10 I haven't had a text message from Lucy .... she changed schools.

4 Complete the text with the correct form of the verbs in brackets.

A Bassington restaurant owner was surprised on Saturday when the famous chef, Zaza Gabon, [1] .... (walk) in for dinner. Bruno Aires, the owner, [2] .... (say), 'She [3] .... (come) in at about 8 pm with another lady who I [4] .... (see) around Bassington recently. They [5] .... (eat) fish and chips.'

Zaza Gabon [6] .... (write) many cook books and [7] .... (appear) on TV shows. She [8] .... (live) in South Africa for the first 20 years of her life until she [9] .... (meet) the film star, Josh Henderson. They [10] .... (live) in the UK since 2012.

5 🎯 Choose the correct sentence in each pair.

1 a Since I saw the film I wanted it.
  b Since I saw the film I have wanted it.

2 a I've known him for 2 years.
  b I've known him since 2 years.

3 a I received your letter yesterday.
  b I've received your letter yesterday.

4 a I haven't talked to you since years!
  b I haven't talked to you for years!

5 a How long have you know your friend?
  b How long have you known your friend?

VOCABULARY *look, taste, smell*

1 Complete the sentences with the correct form of *look, taste* or *smell*.

1 That apple pie .... good. I like the way you have put apples on the top too.

2 I think we should check on the food. It .... as if it's burning.

3 This peach .... delicious. Would you like one?

4 This milk .... a bit sour. I don't think I'll drink it.

5 Dinner .... good – what are we having?

6 You've made the sushi .... so attractive!

2 Complete the conversation with the correct form of *look, taste* or *smell.*

A: I went to the new restaurant in town last night. It was good.

B: It always ¹ .... nice. What did you have?

A: An amazing Thai curry which ² .... beautiful and ³ .... delicious.

B: Did you have a dessert?

A: I did. It was a cake and I didn't know what was in it but I thought I could ⁴ .... coconut, and when I ⁵ .... it I was right!

B: It sounds great – maybe we should go there together.

A: Good idea!

LISTENING

1 Write the letters in the correct order to make breakfast foods.

1 KMIL ....
2 CREALE ....
3 STOAT ....
4 AMJ ....
5 ATE ....
6 CUIEJ ....
7 FUIRT ....

2 ▶10 Listen to the first part of a radio programme where James and Amy are talking about breakfasts around the world. Write the countries you hear in the order you hear them.

1 ....
2 ....
3 ....
4 ....
5 ....

3 Look at these sentences and decide whether a noun (N) or adjective (A) is needed in each space. Write *N* or *A* at the end of each sentence.

1 Amy Haversham has written an article about .... around the world. ....

2 In France, many people eat bread and .... for breakfast. ....

3 The first meal of the day in India might be curry, which is ....

4 Amy says that the Brazilian cheese bread should be .... when you eat it. ....

5 Amy thinks that eating breakfast is a .... thing. ....

6 James suggests trying some .... for breakfast if you don't like cereal. ....

4 ▶11 Listen to the full conversation and complete the sentences in exercise 3 with one word in each space.

5 ▶11 Listen again. Who says each sentence? Write *James* or *Amy.*

1 I usually begin with a glass of fruit juice. ....

2 Tell us more. ....

3 In the UK many people enjoy cereal, which is often sweet. ....

4 Hmm, no, I don't. ....

5 It's delicious! ....

6 How important is breakfast? ....

7 Your brain works better if it isn't thinking 'I need to eat!' ....

8 I'd like to open this up to our listeners. ....

VOCABULARY   Health and illness

1 Write the letters in the correct order to make words and label the robot.

NICH
LEWBO
GNIERF
NALEK
DESHOURL
NEKE
ROTHAT
BUMTH
ROFEDEAH
TEO

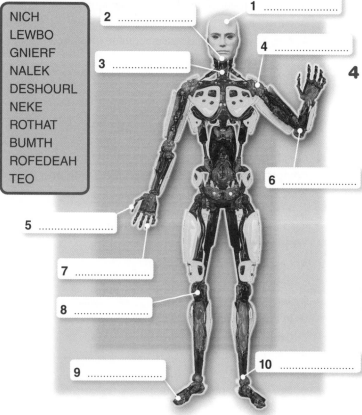

1 ....
2 ....
3 ....
4 ....
5 ....
6 ....
7 ....
8 ....
9 ....
10 ....

2 Choose the correct word.

1 I can hardly speak – my *shoulder / throat* really hurts.
2 I fell and hurt my *thumb / ankle* and now I can't walk.
3 Ibrahim fell on his face in the playground and cut his *toe / chin*.
4 Dad fell off his horse and hurt his *shoulder / forehead*. He can't move his arm very well.
5 Billy is always falling over and hurting his *throat / knees*.
6 Mary can't play the piano because she injured her *finger / toe*.
7 My brother's broken his *thumb / throat* so he can't play tennis today.
8 I didn't see the shelf and I walked straight into it. I've cut my *forehead / elbow*.
9 I have to go to the dentist because I have *stomach ache / toothache*.
10 I have a bad *chin / cough* – but the medicine tastes disgusting!

3 Match the sentence halves.

1 I've got   ....   a   her nose.
2 My throat is   ....   b   on my finger.
3 I've got a high   c   sore.
4 I've got a cut   ....   d   fever.
5 My legs   ....   e   a bad cold.
6 Julie broke   ....   f   ache.

4 Complete the text with the words in the box.

> ache   earache   fever   flu   headache
> stomach ache   temperature   throat

Last year I had a maths test and I hadn't studied, so I didn't want to go to school. I told Mum that my stomach hurt.

'Mum, I've got [1] .... I don't think I can go to school.'

She said, 'Get up and have your breakfast.'

I put my hands over my ears. 'Mum, I've got really bad [2] .... too'.

'Eat your breakfast,' she said. 'You might feel better after breakfast.'

But I didn't eat anything.

'My arms and legs [3] ...., Mum, and my [4] .... is sore. I've got a [5] .... I held my head in my hands as I spoke. I think I've got [6] ...., Mum. I feel awful! I don't think I can go to school today'.

She said, 'Hmm, OK, let's go to the doctor's.'

So we went to the doctor's. He examined me and took my [7] .... Then he said to my mum, 'Tom has a really high [8] .... It's 40 °C. Give him this medicine and he must stay in bed for a week. No computers, no books and no TV. Just rest.'

I didn't understand, I mean I wasn't really ill!

Posted 6.59 pm

READING

1 Read the article quickly and tick (✔) the ideas that are mentioned.

1 What to do if you hurt yourself
2 Taking the right medicines
3 Preparing your body before you exercise
4 How important your mind is
5 Eating the right foods
6 Getting into good habits when you are young

BODY AND MIND

Everybody knows that exercise is good for you. But what about exercise of the mind – how can that help you? *Teenage Mag* spoke to Dr Bathurst, a yoga teacher, about the benefits of yoga.

TM: Many people think that yoga is a slow, boring activity. Tell us why it isn't.

Dr B: Well, yoga is about body and mind. Your mind and your body are working together, and it can be quite fast too. You can't always see that though. You stretch your body, you know, make it longer, and you do the same with your mind. In yoga, you have to get your body into some difficult positions, for example, standing on one foot and moving your whole body forward. Your mind can help you do this. If you look at one place and just think about that, then it's easier. This is something you can learn to do. For young people, who enjoy sport, yoga can help them think, you know, concentrate. In football, for example, people are always shouting at you and telling you what to do. If you can concentrate, then you have a better chance of scoring a goal. Yoga can help with school studies too.

TM: And can it help if you're ill? If you break your arm, or if you get toothache?

Dr B: Well, then you have to go to the doctor or the dentist, but if you know how to relax, you'll get better faster.

TM: And yoga can help you avoid some injuries, can't it?

Dr B: Yes. It's perhaps more important with older people but it's good to get used to it when you're younger. Before you exercise you should always warm up. This is so that your body is warm and you can stretch more without hurting yourself.

TM: Thank you very much! Here at *Teenage Mag* we're going to all try out a yoga class.

Comments

I love yoga, or any of these activities. It's really important to be able to concentrate.

Celine, Switzerland

My basketball coach makes us do warm-up exercises before we have a match. He always shouts out 'You'll play better if you stretch!' Now I understand why!

Herbie, Argentina

This is true. My friend injured her ankle and the doctor said that it was because she hadn't warmed up properly.

Quentin, Mexico

2 **Read the article again and choose the correct word.**

1 Dr Bathurst is a *yoga instructor / dentist*.
2 Yoga is *not as slow as / slower than* people think according to Dr Bathurst.
3 He says people who do yoga *learn how to concentrate / are good at sports*.
4 People who do yoga may *get well sooner / take longer to get well* than people who don't.
5 Yoga can help you because you *prepare your body / test your body* for activity.

3 **Who does these things? Write *Celine*, *Herbie* or *Quentin*.**

1 writes about something that happened to somebody else ....
2 prepares for sport by exercising first ....
3 enjoys activities that are similar to yoga ....

4 **Match the words to the meanings.**

1 benefit .... a think very carefully about something you are doing and nothing else
2 concentrate .... b become happy and comfortable because nothing is worrying you
3 relax .... c something that helps you or gives you an advantage
4 avoid .... d do gentle exercise to prepare for hard exercise
5 warm up .... e stop something from happening or someone from doing something

EP Word profile *for*

Complete the sentences using a phrase with *for*. Choose from the words in brackets.

1 I'm sure there'll be lots of books .... in the second-hand shop. (fun/sale)
2 My friends and I took lots of silly photos, just ....! (fun/instance)
3 Do you know .... that Harry will be at the party on Saturday? (ever/sure)
4 When you're a small kid, you think the holidays will go on ....! (ever/sale)
5 Will we be able to play sports at summer camp – baseball and tennis, ...? (ever/instance)
6 We're going on holiday to the USA .... this summer. (month/sale)
7 Can you tell me the Italian word ....? (ever/cough)

GRAMMAR will and *be going to*

1 Write the words in the correct order to make sentences.

1 We're / 6 pm / to / dinner / going / have / at

....

2 going / to / Josie's / her / in / Grandma / hospital / visit / after school

....

3 will / teacher / give / our / a tennis lesson / us / today / I hope

....

4 she'll / Mum / up / pick us / football practice / after / says

....

5 operation / leg / to / an / is / have / her / on / Stephanie / going

....

6 in here / hot / the window / a bit / I'll / open / It's / so

....

7 party / I'll / some / I think / to / your / pizza / bring

....

8 in / a / competition / are / our / to / school / All the boys / enter / going

....

2 Complete the conversation with the correct form of *will* or *going to*.

Mrs Jones: Edite, we ¹.............................. take you to hospital. Then a doctor can look at your knee.

Edite: Who ².............................. take me, Mrs Jones?

Mrs Jones: I can, but would you like a friend to come too?

Edite: Yes please. My brother Rufus. I'm sure he ³.............................. want to come.

Mrs. Jones: OK, I ⁴.............................. go and fetch him from class. Oh, look, there's Maisie!

Maisie: Hi Mrs Jones. Edite, are you OK?

Edite: I fell over and Mrs Jones ⁵.............................. take me to hospital, Maisie. Can you get Rufus please?

Maisie: Sure, I ⁶.............................. text him now. And I ⁷.............................. pick up all your things.

Edite: Thanks, Maisie. I ⁸.............................. miss our English lesson – can you take notes please?

Maisie: Sure!

3 Complete the short conversations with the correct form of *will* or *going to*.

A: What ¹.............................. (you/do) after school?

B: Mum and I ².............................. (look) in the shopping mall for a new pair of shoes.

A: Your phone's ringing. Would you like me to get it for you?

B: No it's OK. I ³.............................. (not/answer) it now. I ⁴.............................. (check) it later.

A: Bobbie ⁵.............................. (have) a birthday party. ⁶.............................. (you/go)?

B: I don't know. I think I ⁷.............................. (stay) at home and watch TV.

A: ⁸.............................. (help) me with my homework, Mum?

B: I can't, but your Dad ⁹.............................. (explain) it to you. He loved maths when he was a child!

4 Complete the conversation with the correct form of the verbs in the box. Use *will* or *going to*.

ask	be	drive	get
go	look	stay	take

Sasha is at home with a fever. Her mum is talking to her.

'OK, I ¹.............................. you to the doctor's this morning.'

'Oh, really, Mum. It ².............................. away.'

'No, I've decided. The doctor ³.............................. at you and make sure it's nothing serious. I ⁴.............................. for some medicine for your cough, Sasha.'

'Urgh! I hate that medicine! It tastes disgusting!'

'I know, but I want you to get better.'

'OK, Mum. But ⁵.............................. in town? I just want to be in bed. I feel ill.'

'I know, but the doctor can't give you medicine without seeing you. I ⁶.............................. my car keys and we ⁷.............................. in now. I don't think it ⁸.............................. very busy now.'

5 👁 Correct the mistakes in these sentences or tick (✔) any you think are correct.

1 It's sunny next Saturday.

....

2 I know we're going to have an awesome time!

....

3 Tomorrow, we will go to the cinema to see the best film of the year, 'New moon'.

....

4 I enjoy spending time with her because they're moments that are not going to be happened again.

....

5 I like him because we talk a lot about what are we going to do.

....

VOCABULARY   Illnesses and injuries: verbs

1 Choose the correct verb.

1 Fran *caught* / *broke* a really bad cold recently.
2 I can't concentrate. My head *hurts* / *feels*.
3 Maggie fell off her bike and *had* / *broke* her arm.
4 The athlete has *injured* / *got* his knee so he can't take part in the race.
5 The little boy fell over and *felt* / *cut* both of his elbows.
6 Are you *feeling* / *getting* OK? Sit down here.

2 Complete the text with the correct form of the verbs in the box. Use each verb once.

> be   break   catch   cut   feel
> get   have   hurt   injure

Something ¹............................. wrong with everyone in my class at the moment! Jessica fell over in basketball and ²............................. her knee. She can walk but it really ³............................. Unfortunately, Sam wasn't so lucky. He also fell over and he has ⁴............................. his arm. Mary isn't at school because she ⁵............................. flu. We think she ⁶............................. it from Fred who came back to school yesterday. Monica was cooking something last week and she ⁷............................. her finger with a knife.

I hope everyone ⁸............................. better soon but I don't ⁹............................. very well myself!

WRITING   A story

See Prepare to write box, Student's Book page 35.

1 Read the story below quickly. Choose the best title.

1 The worst day of my life
2 A fantastic cycling holiday
3 A difficult friend

> It was a beautiful day. My friend Sally and I went on a bike ride. We prepared a picnic lunch and we cycled to our friend's house. We had to cycle up a steep hill. It was hard to get to the top but we managed. Then we went down the other side. We went really fast. It was so much fun! Unfortunately, I didn't see a stone on the road and I fell off my bike. I landed on my arm. I don't remember any more. I woke up in hospital. I broke my arm in three places. I spent most of my holiday in bed.
>
> By Pedro A.

2 Read the story again. Decide if the information is from the beginning (B), the middle (M) or the end (E).

1 going down the hill   ....
2 the weather   ....
3 how difficult the hill was   ....
4 falling off the bike   ....
5 how Pedro felt about the holiday ....
6 people in the story   ....

3 Divide the story into three parts – beginning, middle and end. Write the first three words of the middle and end parts.

....
....

4 These sentences are from different stories. Decide if they are from the beginning (B), the middle (M) or the end (E) of the story.

1 We had a wonderful time!   ....
2 It was a rainy day and we had nothing to do.   ....
3 Meg screamed. She was frightened.   ....
4 In the end, everything was OK.   ....
5 Mum asked me to do some shopping for her.   ....
6 Finally I understood what she said! ....

5 You are going to write a story. Look at the picture. It is from the middle of the story. Answer these questions.

1 Who is telling the story?
....
2 What was the woman doing before she fell?
....
3 What happened to her?
....
4 Is the woman alone, or with someone?
....
5 Where are they now?
....
5 How does the story end?
....

6 Now write your story

• Write about 100 words.
• Remember to check your spelling and grammar.

VOCABULARY   Animals

1 Add the missing vowels (A, E, I, O, U, Y) to complete these animal words.

1 G .... R .... FF ....
2 B .... T
3 D .... NK .... Y
4 .... NT
5 C .... M L
6 B .... TT .... RFLY
7 K .... NG .... R ....
8 B .... R
9 FR .... G
10 D .... LPH .... N
11 B ....
12 M .... SQ .... T ....
13 P .... RR .... T
14 T .... G .... R
15 SH .... RK
16 WH .... L ....
17 SN .... K ....
18 P .... NG .... N
19 FL ....
20 R .... T

2 Complete the puzzle and find the hidden animal. Which animal …

1 lives in the ocean and has very sharp teeth?
2 is very small and can be black or red?
3 is small and flies at night?
4 can't jump without using its tail?
5 is a kind of large cat?

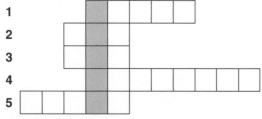

Hidden word: ....

3 Read these descriptions. Which animal is it?

1 ....

I've always loved these animals. They're very intelligent and fantastic swimmers. They live in the sea and they play – they jump out of the water and sometimes they swim with people in the water.

2 ....

These animals like hot weather! They live in the desert and in Arabic there are about 160 words for this animal because they are so important. They travel and carry things and people. They are quiet, calm animals but they do get angry sometimes.

3 ....

These insects are often really pretty. They have beautiful wings but they cannot fly if their body temperature is less than 30 °C. So you won't see them on cold days!

4 ....

These birds can't fly. They eat fish and other sea food, and they can see very well under water. They live for about 15–20 years in the wild. They live in very cold places.

4 Match the animals in exercise 3 to the pictures.

1 ....
2 ....
3 ....
4 ....

READING

1 What do you think 'native animal' means?

1 an animal that is from a certain part of the world
2 an animal that lives in many different places
3 an animal that stays in the same place all its life

2 Read the article and choose the correct answer,
A, B, C or D.

1 What is the writer doing in this article?
  A complaining about a wildlife organisation
  B describing what a wildlife organisation does
  C reporting an interview with an animal expert
  D giving advice about how to look after pets
2 What does the writer say about WIRES?
  A The courses they provide are rather disappointing.
  B The visits they make to farms in the area are helpful.
  C They should explain how they look after the animals.
  D They are doing a very important job in Australia.
3 What does Guy's dad do for the organisation?
  A He tries to save animals that are hurt.
  B He answers the phone at the WIRES office.
  C He chooses someone to go and see the animal.
  D He prepares the special clothes for WIRES helpers.
4 What happened to the baby bat?
  A It was injured by other bats.
  B It is now looked after by Guy at home.
  C It lived and was put back into the wild.
  D It is still living at the animal centre.
5 What would someone working for WIRES say?

  A We can send someone out quickly to help your pet in your home or farm.

  B If you see a snake, a bat or another wild animal in danger, call us immediately.

  C We are a new organisation in Australia that looks after all kinds of animals.

  D If you want to have a career with us, you must attend at least one of our courses.

3 Match the highlighted words in the article to their meanings.

1 look after someone or something ....
2 saw something and became interested in it ....
3 save someone or something from a dangerous situation ....
4 hurt after an accident ....
5 arrange and run an event ....

This month Angelina Horsefield writes about an animal rescue society in Australia: WIRES

WIRES (Wildlife Information and Rescue Service) began in 1985 when someone found an injured bird in a park in Sydney, Australia. At the time, no one knew how to help this 'native' animal. WIRES help animals like snakes, kangaroos and, of course, birds. However, they can only help Australian wildlife, so they can't help other animals like cats or rabbits.

Like other animal rescue groups, WIRES need more people. I believe they are definitely helping the local animals, but they can only continue if others join in. They hold excellent courses, where people can learn what to do when they find an injured animal. They also explain what happens to the animals in their care. Many of the people who help also take care of the animals themselves in their own gardens or on their farms.

I spoke to 15-year-old Guy McKenzie, whose dad helps WIRES in his free time. Guy told me about the work they do. 'Dad usually gets a phone call at home and drives immediately to where the animal is, to rescue it. He has special equipment and always wears gloves. The animals are wild, after all!'

Guy also talked about a woman who found a bat in her garden. She thought it might be dead but then she noticed that there was a baby bat too. Guy's dad brought it back to the centre, where it grew into a healthy adult. Then, WIRES were able to return it to nature. Guy showed me a baby kangaroo that his dad was looking after and told me that one day he'll be doing the same thing. Yes, he will, for sure.

● ○ ●   READ MORE ▶

GRAMMAR Modals of probability

1 Complete the conversation with *might, must, can't* or *could.*

A: What's that? Oh, I know, it ¹ .... be a big cat.

B: Hmm, I don't think so. It ² .... be an elephant because it's too small.

A: Right, but it's an African animal. It ³ .... be a rhino but it's the wrong colour.

B: I know! It ⁴ .... be a giraffe – look at its skin!

2 Choose the correct answer.

1 I .... watch a programme about animals tonight.
   a might   **b** can't

2 That .... be the longest snake I've ever seen!
   a can't   **b** must

3 Phil .... be ill because he isn't at school today.
   a might   **b** can't

4 It .... be a parrot. It's the wrong colour!
   a can't   **b** must

5 I know you've lost your book. .... this be it?
   a Can't   **b** Could

6 You .... be really excited – you have tickets for your favourite band!
   a must   **b** could

7 Taylor .... call me later but she's not sure.
   a must   **b** might

8 I'm tired. It .... be time for bed.
   a must   **b** can't

3 Complete the sentences with the correct modal verb. Sometimes more than one answer is possible.

1 I think it .... rain today – look at the sky.

2 This .... be for me – I don't like this kind of magazine.

3 You .... be happy with your wonderful exam results!

4 That animal .... bite you – watch out!

5 My little sister is in a bad mood but she .... be hungry.

6 Everyone's wearing hats and coats. It .... be very cold.

7 I can't find my books but they .... be at school.

8 It .... be Adele playing the piano. She plays better than that.

4 Complete the sentences with the correct modal verb. Sometimes more than one answer is possible.

A: What are you reading? And what is *that?*

B: It's an amazing animal. It ¹ .... be very clever, it's a type of ant.

A: Right! It ² .... be from Europe! Look at those trees and the background!

B: No, I think it ³ .... be from South America somewhere. I haven't finished reading it yet!

A: Well, I ⁴ .... do my 'wonderful animals' project about this! Can I have the magazine?

5 👁 Choose the correct sentence in each pair.

1 **a** I think this can be difficult to do.
   b I think this might be difficult to do.

2 **a** They must be beautiful!
   b They might to be beautiful!

3 **a** I thought that you might want to come to my house to play the game with me.
   b I thought that you want to come to my house to play the game with me.

4 **a** I'm imagining your new house and it might be wonderful.
   b I'm imagining your new house and it must be wonderful.

5 **a** I thought that the exhibition about the future of your city must be very nice.
   b I thought that the exhibition about the future of your city might be very nice.

VOCABULARY Adverbs of probability

1 Write the words in the correct order to make sentences.

1 is / This / not / definitely / cat / my

....

2 your brother / Perhaps / help / with / your work / can / you

....

3 probably / a / That / famous painting / is / very

....

4 probably / to / tomorrow / the dolphins / going / We're / see

....

5 phone / definitely / are / Mum and Dad / buy / going to / another / me / not

....

6 not / over there / but / the bears / I'm / are / sure / Perhaps

....

2 Choose the correct word to complete the text.

definitely   definitely not   perhaps   probably

This is photo that my mum gave me. No one really knows much about it. It is ¹............................ old. It's a photo of a man and it's ²............................ my mum's grandfather. He looks young in the photo, so ³............................ it was before he married my grandmother. It's ⁴............................ easy to tell because the photo is damaged.

LISTENING

1 You are going to hear a girl called Kate talking about a story she wrote for a competition. Tick (✔) the questions you think you will hear.

1 What's your full name? ☐
2 Can you tell us something about your story? ☐
3 Why did you write about fish? ☐
4 What's your favourite animal? ☐
5 Why did you enter the competition? ☐

2 ▶12 Listen and check your answers.

3 ▶12 Listen again and choose the correct answer.

1 What is Kate's story about?
  a why a boy and his parents moved to London
  b how a teenage boy enjoys being with his animals
2 Kate wrote about fish because
  a they are her favourite animals.
  b she looks after some for her mother.
3 Why did Kate enter the competition?
  a Her teacher asked her to.
  b She wanted a new challenge.
4 Marco is
  a an unhappy boy.
  b a boy who enjoys fishing.
5 What does Kate do to relax?
  a She writes more stories.
  b She spends time in the countryside.

4 The picture is about Kate's story. Tick (✔) the sentences that are correct.

1 I can see a boy. He's looking at the fish. ☐
2 There's a window in the background and we can see the countryside. ☐
3 There are three people in the picture and the one on the right is taking a picture. ☐
4 On the right there's a table and on the left there is a bookcase. ☐
5 The boy is probably looking at the fish because he likes them. ☐
6 The fish might be hungry. Perhaps he's going to give them some food. ☐

VOCABULARY Adjectives: feelings

1 Find twelve adjectives in the word square (→ ↓).

D	H	E	L	P	F	U	L	W	R	S	E
I	E	L	L	D	O	N	C	E	E	T	M
S	P	R	O	U	D	T	O	X	L	R	B
A	B	C	Z	N	B	L	N	W	A	E	A
P	K	D	W	Y	X	A	F	M	X	S	R
P	J	J	L	T	Q	Z	U	F	E	S	R
O	K	D	N	L	T	Y	S	M	D	E	A
I	C	O	N	F	I	D	E	N	T	D	S
N	J	Y	Q	D	R	T	D	M	R	N	S
T	V	R	D	N	L	O	N	E	L	Y	E
E	K	C	R	E	A	T	I	V	E	M	D
D	E	X	H	A	U	S	T	E	D	K	D

2 Write the words from the word square next to their meanings.

1 willing to help, or useful ....
2 feeling very pleased about something you have done ....
3 unhappy because you are not with other people ....
4 not able to think clearly or to understand something ....
5 describes someone who doesn't like working or using any effort ....
6 unhappy because someone or something was not as good as you hoped ....
7 very tired ....
8 producing or using original and unusual ideas ....
9 feeling happy because nothing is worrying you ....
10 certain about your ability to do things well ....
11 worried and not able to relax ....
12 feeling ashamed or shy ....

3 Complete the sentences with the adjectives from the box. There is one adjective you don't need.

> confident   confused   creative
> disappointed   embarrassed   exhausted
> lazy   lonely   proud   relaxed   stressed

1 Danny is .... that he'll pass the exam – he's studied so hard.
2 I don't understand what you're saying – I'm ....
3 Alison didn't get what she wanted for her birthday; she's a bit ....
4 Jack does yoga because it makes him feel ....
5 I'm so .... of our school – we won the competition.
6 I did nothing yesterday – I felt really ....
7 Pedro felt .... when he had to speak in front of the whole class.
8 Eva is .... – she paints, writes and she's musical too!
9 I've been running for half an hour and now I feel completely .... !
10 Carol is feeling .... because she has a test tomorrow and she's working hard.

4 Choose the two answers that are possible in each sentence.

1 Emma usually gets the best marks in class and she's sure she will win first prize again. But if you don't understand the work, she explains it.
   a confident   **b** lonely   **c** helpful

2 Mrs Paderewski has worked many hours recently. She bought a new computer and she went on an expensive holiday. She had to work hard to pay for it.
   a embarrassed   **b** exhausted   **c** stressed

3 Jackson isn't very happy at the moment. He spends a lot of time on his own. I don't think he likes it. Also, I know that he wasn't happy with his maths result last week.
   a lonely   **b** proud   **c** disappointed

4 We sometimes play a game at home and I don't always remember the answers. I go red! Last night we played and there was so much noise I couldn't think properly. But it's only a game!
   a embarrassed   **b** confused   **c** lazy

5 Jan passed all his exams and is going to university to study geography. His parents are very pleased. Now he's going to have a rest over the summer.
   a proud   **b** relaxed   **c** confident

READING

1 Read the text about mood rings quickly. What makes their colour change?

1 your mood   **2** your body temperature   **3** the weather

2 Read the text again and add the correct questions (a–d) to the paragraphs (1–3). There is one question you don't need.

a So how do they work?
b But do they really work?
c Where do they work best?
d How are you feeling today?

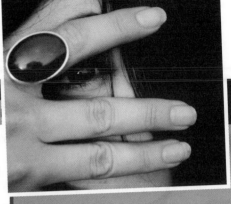

From the past

| About | Stones | Pu... |

1 ....

Do you feel relaxed? Or stressed? Or maybe you've just received some good news and you are confident. Or maybe you don't know? It doesn't matter because a mood ring will be able to tell you how you're feeling, and in an attractive way. Mood rings have been around since the 1970s when they were invented. Then they became fashion items especially with teens. People usually wore them as rings on their fingers, but there were other jewellery items too, such as necklaces.

2 ....

Mood rings are made of a special kind of stone which changes because of your body temperature. So if your body is hot, then they will be a different colour than if your body is cold. If you are happy, then your body temperature increases and the ring turns blue. But if you are stressed or excited then the blood flows towards your heart, and so away from your fingers, and the mood ring changes to yellow. In very cold weather, it becomes black.

3 ....

Not really. It's true that they change colour according to your temperature. However, your body changes temperature for many reasons – not just your mood. You might be really excited, but if you are standing outside and it's freezing cold, the ring will be blue! So they are not reliable and people soon realised that. However, they are a fun gift because they really do change colour.

Comments:

My mum read this and she showed me her mood ring that she got when she was a kid. It's in the shape of a bird and she loved it. It was black when we took it out of the drawer and then she put it on and it turned yellow! I think that's amazing after 40 years.
Jocelyn, Launceston, Tasmania

This is great. I have to do a science project on 'change' and so this is perfect! I've just been into town and bought one too. It's yellowy green at the moment – probably because I'm feeling confident!
Harry, Vancouver, Canada

3 Read the text again. Are these sentences true (T) or false (F)?

1 A mood ring is a fun item that can tell the future.   ....
2 In the 1970s, it was mostly young people who wore them.   ....
3 The colours for happy and excited moods are different.   ....
4 If you are outside on a snowy day, the mood ring is probably green.   ....
5 Jocelyn's mum's mood ring only shows one colour now.   ....
6 Harry is going to show his class a mood ring.   ....

EP Word profile *time*

Choose the correct answer.

1 You must arrive .... every day.
   a on time   **b** in time   **c** time.

2 That woman is strange – .... I see her she looks odd.
   a in time   **b** every time   **c** at the same time

3 Have you got .... for a coffee?
   a in time   **b** on time   **c** time

4 OK, ... for the last class of the day! Hurray!
   a on time   **b** in time   **c** time

5 It takes .... to get from one side of Australia to the other.
   a a long time   **b** in time   **c** on time

6 I love wearing a dress and boots ....
   a time   **b** in time   **c** at the same time

7 I won't be back .... to see Bill, so can you say hello for me please?
   a on time   **b** in time   **c** at the same time

GRAMMAR *just, already* and *yet*

1 **Write the words in the correct order to make sentences.**

1 hasn't / The / yet / started / film

....

2 has / photos / just / uploaded / Shelly / the

....

3 finished / He's / game / that / already

....

4 out / have / Dad / gone / and / just / Mum

....

5 already / my / I've / done / homework

....

6 go / to / I'm / ready / yet / not / out

....

2 **Match the questions to the answers.**

1 Have you finished that work already? ....

2 Do I have to take my shoes off? ....

3 Do you want to go to the cinema? ....

4 Has anyone heard from Becky? ....

5 Have you managed to buy the tickets yet? ....

6 What's happened? ....

a No, I've already seen the film three times.

b Yes, I've just cleaned the floor!

c No, I think we're too late.

d My team have just won their first game!

e Yes, it was really easy.

f No, she hasn't texted yet. I'll call her now.

3 **Choose the correct words to complete the blog entry.**

Hi guys!!

I'm really proud of everyone. I've ¹ *just / already* read the news on our social media page. It's great that we're having a party for the whole school. We've ² *already / yet* planned the food and lots of people have ³ *already / just* replied to our invitations. But does anyone know why some of the kids in Mr Barker's class haven't replied ⁴ *yet / already*? Eric Styles has been really helpful and is going to find out who hasn't received an invitation ⁵ *yet / just*. He thinks there's an email problem with that class.

Has anyone thought about the music ⁶ *just / yet*? Let's talk about that at the next meeting. I've ⁷ *yet / just* sent the people who are organising it a text message – so check your phones.

Tina K.

— — — — — — — — — — — — —

End of Year Party Club

4 **Complete the sentences with *just, already* or *yet*.**

1 I've .... had dinner – about 10 minutes ago!

2 I haven't finished reading that book ....

3 We weren't expecting them until 6 o'clock but they've .... arrived!

4 Mum said she has .... sent a text. Check your phone.

5 Sally's .... gone to the library – Mum's taken her.

6 Mr Bentley hasn't given us our homework ....

7 I've .... seen this film – I went with Barry last week.

8 Dad hasn't finished on the computer ....

9 The train has .... left – right on time!

10 Have you been to the new sports centre .... ? I went yesterday and it's really great!

5 **Complete Sandrine's part in the conversation and add the words in brackets.**

1 **Sandrine:** you / see / the news / ? / I / see / it / ! (just)

....

Leon: It's fabulous news isn't it? Our favourite band's coming to our town!

2 **Sandrine:** they / announce / tour dates / ? (yet)

....

Leon: No, but sometime in March I think. Let's text Marek.

3 **Sandrine:** he / see / the news / ? (already)

....

Leon: Yes, because he's at football practice at the moment. How exciting!

6 ⊙ **Correct the mistakes in these sentences or tick (✔) any you think are correct.**

1 I just have found a very interesting game online.

....

2 I haven't seen yet my house.

....

3 I haven't already bought a book to take on holiday – what do you think I should take?

....

4 I have just got a new computer game.

....

5 We have alredy decided that you should bring a cake.

....

VOCABULARY Adjectives: -ed or -ing

1 Choose the correct adjective.

1 Maggie is doing her homework and she's *bored* / *boring*.

2 I hate it when my mum asks me about school – it's so *annoying* / *annoyed*.

3 Dad was *shocking* / *shocked* when he heard the news.

4 It was *surprising* / *surprised* that Anne won the game so easily.

5 I'm a bit *confused* / *confusing* about the ending of the book – what actually happened?

6 Johnny stood up in class but forgot what to say – he was *embarrassing* / *embarrassed*.

7 We went to bed early last night because we were *tiring* / *tired*.

8 This new video game is *disappointing* / *disappointed*.

9 This film is really *bored* / *boring* – I think I'll read a book instead.

10 Were you *surprised* / *surprising* to hear that Joe won first prize in the competition?

WRITING A story

See Prepare to write box, Student's Book page 57.

1 Read the story. Choose the best first sentence.

1 Joe took a picture of the painting.

2 Joe stood beside his painting and looked at the camera.

3 Joe wanted to paint a picture of his cat.

He smiled. 'Thank you,' said the photographer. Everyone was really pleased. 'You've just won first prize! How do you feel?' asked Maggie, his best friend. 'I'm not sure. I'm exhausted – it was a lot of hard work for a long time, but I'm really proud! I didn't think I could do it!' Joe painted pictures in his free time and he enjoyed painting pictures of his own animals. Everyone wanted to know about his next painting. He said he didn't know but actually he did. He was already thinking about the beautiful colours of his horse.

2 Underline the verbs in the story in these tenses.

1 the past simple

2 the present perfect

3 the past continuous

4 the present simple

2 Complete the text with the words from the box. There is one word you don't need.

annoying   bored   boring   confused
embarrassed   embarrassing   shocked
surprised

Robin picked up the piece of paper and started to read it. She was [1]................................ to learn that Jerry didn't like his new computer game. Then she heard a noise. She was [2]................................ because she was reading Jerry's personal letter to his friend.
The door opened and Jerry came in 'I'm really [3]................................ that you come into my room, Robin. It's very [4].................................' Robin stood up and said, 'I was [5]................................. Let's play your new computer game.' 'Yes, let's!' said Jerry, sitting down at the computer. Robin was [6]................................ – perhaps the letter wasn't true. How [7]................................ !

3 Rewrite these sentences so that they mean the same, using words from the story.

1 I'm very tired.
....

2 I don't know.
....

3 Everyone was really happy.
....

4 He liked painting pictures of his animals.
....

5 Everyone asked questions about his next painting.
....

4 Your English teacher has asked you to write a story. Your story must begin with this sentence:

Jack opened the email and smiled.

• Write about 100 words.

• Remember to check your grammar and spelling.

VOCABULARY TV, films and literature

1 Write the letters in the correct order to make entertainment words.

1 RHOORR MFIL ....
2 DIATNMAE MFIL ....
3 STRIOICHAL RAADM ....
4 ATICON MFIL ....
5 VOLE RYOST ....
6 TRIERLLH ....
7 TACH OHWS ....
8 MDCTNUEARYO ....
9 DEMURR SYMETRY ....
10 CODMEY ....
11 POAS POERA ....
12 CISECEN FINTIOC ....

2 Choose the type of film from exercise 1.

1
....
This is a story about a boy and a girl. They see each other and they like each other. Then the boy has to move to a different country but the girl still loves him. A great movie and you'll cry at the end!

2
....
This is a film about a superhero and the things he has to do to save the world. At the beginning, it's really exciting but then it's boring. You hear the actors' voices but you don't see them because they are cartoons.

3
....
This takes place on a big cruise ship with a lot of people. Suddenly, one person dies and then the story begins. One of the people on the ship starts to look for the killer. It's a really good story and it keeps you guessing until the end.

4
....
I love these kinds of programmes, especially the ones about nature and animals. The photography is usually excellent too. I saw one last night about the secret world of spiders!

5
....
This story takes place in the year 3014 when the world is a very different place. Our hero, a boy aged 16, receives an object from the past from his father. He wants to find out more about it and so he travels back in time. I don't really like this type of film but it was quite interesting.

6
....
This takes place in 1900. There is a war and life is very hard. The men are fighting and the women are looking after children and the people who are hurt. It's a traditional story, you know, men and women, I love films like this – you see that life was really hard in the past.

3 Complete the conversations with the words in the boxes.

| action   comedy   horror |

A: Did you see the film last night?
B: Yes, it was great! All those fast car scenes – a real 1 .... film.
A: Oh, I thought it was a funny film – you know a 2 ....
B: True! and it was also a bit scary, so also a 3 .... film!
A: Yes, it was three films in one!

| historical   love story   thriller |

A: Let's take this DVD. It takes place in London in 1920.
B: Oh no, that's boring. That's my mum's favourite – a 4 .... drama.
A: OK, but here it says it's a 5 .... – so really exciting.
B: Oh, is it also a 6 .... – you know, boy meets girl? Yuck! I hate films like that.

| documentary   science fiction   soap opera |

A: Did you see the film last night?
B: *Star Wars*? Of course! I love it! Best 7 .... film ever.
A: I know. Did you see the 8 .... after it about how they wrote the story?
B: No, Mum wanted to watch her 9 .... – so boring, about people living in the same street and their lives.

READING

SIT ON A BOOK!

1 Look at the photo. What do you think it is?

1 a seat
2 an advertisement
3 a sculpture

2 Read the text. Answer these questions.

1 What kind of a project was 'Books about Town'?
  a writers reading aloud from their books
  b famous writers visiting London
  c an exhibition about writers and reading books
2 Which of the following was not on the benches?
  a pictures from the authors' homes
  b pictures about the authors' lives
  c pictures from stories that the authors wrote
3 Where could you find the answers to each quiz?
  a by speaking to an author
  b by going online
  c by visiting some of the benches
4 What could you do at the Hercule Poirot bench?
  a buy the author's books
  b meet the man who created the pictures in the books
  c receive a gift from the author
5 What is the author doing in the last paragraph?
  a apologising because the exhibition has ended
  b saying that the exhibition was a good idea
  c thanking the organisers of the exhibition
6 What does Ivan most like?
  a making money for more reading projects
  b looking at all the different benches
  c the fact that the benches will go to another town

3 Match the highlighted words in the text to their meanings.

1 very interested ....
2 a visit to another place for a short time ....
3 in a particular place ....
4 people who admire a person, sport, etc. ....
5 people who appear in a play, film or story ....

4 Complete the sentences with the correct form of the words from exercise 3.

1 I don't like the main .... in this book.
2 The Bradshaws often go on a .... to the city.
3 Rafael is a .... football supporter.
4 The library is .... next to the park.
5 I'm not really a .... of classical music.

London had an interesting book reading project in the summer of 2014. It was called *Books about Town* and it celebrated London's storytellers and stories by inviting you to sit on a book! How can you sit on a book? Read on!

The organisers placed 50 seats, called 'book benches', around the city. Each bench had pictures of the author or the author's stories. The Mary Poppins bench, for example, had a picture of Mary flying through the air with her umbrella. Other famous characters included James Bond, Sherlock Holmes and Hercule Poirot.

With 50 different benches, and stories to discover, there were also four 'trails', or walks, that led to several benches in the same area. You could download a map that showed you where the benches were situated. There was a quiz that went with the trails and you had to answer questions about the different benches and their authors and stories. The answers were on or near the benches. There were also online competitions during the summer while the exhibition was running.

There were events at the benches too. At the James Bond bench, there were free books as presents waiting for keen readers. For Agatha Christie fans, there were some famous people who visited the benches. Her grandson read out part of one of the stories, and the man who drew the pictures for the Agatha Christie novels since the 1970s was also there.

The benches celebrated authors and their stories of all ages. So this was a perfect day trip for the whole family! But the exhibition ended in September, when the benches were sold to raise money for books and reading projects in the UK.

Comments

What a great idea! I really love books and I visited the website – there's a lot of information there. It's a great project, especially because there was a lot of money for reading projects at the end. I really liked the Alex Rider bench. That's one of my favourite stories. I couldn't go because I live in Canada. I hope they do something like that here. Ivan, Vancouver.

EP Word profile *hope*

Complete the text with the correct form of hope.

Do you ¹ .... that you will be rich and famous one day? Zara does and she ² .... to be a famous film star. She knows that sometimes it will seem ³ .... and all she will have is ⁴ .... She's ⁵ .... that a famous director will notice her and ⁶ .... she'll be offered a starring role.

GRAMMAR Relative clauses

1 Choose the two answers that are possible in each sentence.

1 Yesterday I saw a man .... works at the library.
   a who   **b** which   **c** that

2 Tonight we can watch the film .... stars your favourite actor.
   a who   **b** that   **c** which

3 Have you visited the museum .... is in Lark Street?
   a where   **b** which   **c** that

4 The person .... wrote this story has an amazing imagination.
   a who   **b** which   **c** that

5 I find it difficult to read books .... include long descriptions of places.
   a which   **b** that   **c** where

6 My mobile phone is the object .... I love most!
   a that   **b** who   **c** which

2 Choose the correct word.

1 This is a wonderful book *who / that* I'm reading.

2 We went on a tour of the studios in Hollywood *which / where* many famous films were made.

3 Kristen Stewart, *who / which* was in *Snow White and the Huntsman*, is my favourite actress.

4 There's a great site *where / that* you can catch up on TV shows.

5 This is the TV show *which / who* I was telling you about.

6 Some people *which / who* are at my school can be really annoying.

3 Complete the text with the correct relative pronouns.

The Hunger Games is a thrilling story
¹.............................. takes place in another
world. It is about a dangerous competition.
The story is about a girl called Katniss
and her family and friends. In the story,
everyone must watch a terrible competition,
².............................. is shown on TV
³.............................. everyone can see what
is happening. When Primrose,
⁴.............................. is Katniss' sister, is
chosen, Katniss decides to take her place.
In the end, the rules of the competition
change. The book and the film are both
popular with teens. Many teens
⁵.............................. read the book first
wanted to see how different the film was.
Some liked the parts ⁶.............................. the
characters had to make difficult choices.

4 Complete the sentences with an ending from the box and the correct relative pronoun.

takes place on a beach
was in a film about dancing
have Daniel Craig in them
Carole was reading
my Mum and Dad first met
is showing at the City Theatre

1 I enjoy all films ....
2 That is the cinema ....
3 This is a great film ....
4 I love that actress ....
5 This is the book ....
6 Ariana wants to see the play ....

5 👁 Choose the correct sentence in each pair.

1 **a** There is a space which is very clean and suitable for a picnic.
   b There is a space where is very clean and suitable for a picnic.

2 **a** Well, I have a friend that is called Manuel.
   b Well, I have a friend that called Manuel.

3 **a** The only boy let me play with him was Fidel.
   b The only boy who let me play with him was Fidel.

4 **a** I've chosen the park is near your house because it's a quiet place.
   b I've chosen the park which is near your house because it's a quiet place.

5 **a** I got a new computer game that is called Sims 2.
   b I got a new computer game is called Sims 2.

VOCABULARY Easily confused words

1 Choose the correct word.

1 You have to *advise* / *advice* the teacher if you are going to miss school.
2 *Who's* / *Whose* book is this?
3 Janice *past* / *passed* me in the street and didn't say anything!
4 I don't know *whether* / *weather* we're going to see you at the weekend.
5 Did you *lose* / *loose* your key yesterday?
6 Where are they boys? *They're* / *Their* outside.
7 No one can enter the library *except* / *accept* the head.

2 Complete the conversation with the correct word from each pair in the box.

> borrow/lend   bookshop/library   history/story
> notice/realise   remember/remind
> sensible/sensitive

A: Can you ¹............................ me what we have to do for our project?

B: Oh, I didn't ²............................ you weren't there when we talked about it. ³............................ that we looked at countries?

A: Yes. We have to do some research, don't we?

B: That's right, so if you go to the ⁴............................ , they'll ⁵............................ you a book for a week.

A: OK. Does it have to be a ⁶............................ book?

B: No, it can be a ⁷............................ from a different country. Our teacher made a list of 20 books for us to choose from. I didn't ⁸............................ but Alan said that there are only about four left to ⁹............................ . So you need to be quick!

A: OK, and then I have to read it and write about it? Is that right?

B: Yes. Did someone tell you?

A: No, Izzy sent me a text. She's writing about America. But her Mum bought her book for her at the ¹⁰............................ because she wants to keep it at the end of the project.

B: Yes, that's ¹¹............................ .

A: But the story made her cry!

B: Really? Perhaps she's a bit ¹²............................ !

LISTENING

1 Tick (✔) the different places you watch films.

at home ☐
at the cinema ☐
on your phone ☐
on your computer/tablet ☐
other (say where) ☐
....

2 ▶13 Listen to a radio show. The presenter is talking about a film festival. Tick (✔) the information she mentions.

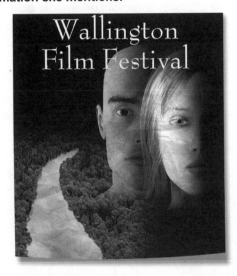

1 the number of films ☐
2 where the films will be shown ☐
3 the price of the tickets ☐
4 when the festival is taking place ☐
5 the person to contact for information ☐
6 where to buy tickets ☐

3 Read the notes. Decide what information you have to find for each note.

> ### Film festival
>
> Festival topic this year: ¹............................
>
> Total number of films at the festival:
> ²............................
>
> Outside screen is near the ³............................
>
> Start time of festival: ⁴............................pm
>
> Name of restaurant for Saturday's event:
> ⁵............................
>
> On Sunday, class available in: ⁶............................

1 **a** place name   **b** subject name
2 **a** number   **b** name
3 **a** place   **b** number
4 **a** name   **b** number
5 **a** restaurant name   **b** event name
6 **a** name of teacher   **b** type of class

4 ▶13 Listen again and complete the notes.

VOCABULARY Computing phrases

1 Add the missing vowels (A, E, I, O, U) to these computing words.

1 D.... L.... T....
2 P.... SSW.... RD
3 L.... NK
4 .... NST LL
5 .... PP
6 P.... DC.... ST
7 SH ...R....
8 F.... L....
9 V.... R.... S
10 D.... WNL........D
11 S........RCH
12 .... PL........D

2 Choose the correct word.

1 Oh, no! I've just *installed / deleted* all my work.
2 You should change your *password / podcast* regularly.
3 Have you listened to Jamie's music *podcast / app*?
4 Don't open that email! There's a *link / virus* in it – it'll destroy everything.
5 My sister is doing a *search / password* for information about the planets for her homework.
6 When you've finished your video, *install / upload* it to the website.
7 I've just bought *a file / an app* that tells me when to go to bed!
8 Mia spends a lot of time *sharing / downloading* her photos on Instagram.

3 Complete the crossword, using the clues below.

Across

1 This might tell you how many hours you've studied!
5 This is usually made up of letters and numbers – and you have to remember it!
6 remove something from a computer's memory
8 put a computer program onto a computer so that the computer can use it

Down

2 You can listen to it on your phone or the internet at any time.
3 This is a program that is secretly put on your computer and can damage it.
4 This can be a document or a short video clip.
7 If you click on this, it takes you to a website.

4 Complete the text with the correct form of the words from exercise 1.

Our school has a website that is only for its students. If you have to ¹s............................ a ²f............................ , you can do it on the website. Each student creates their own ³p............................ and then they can go to the website. Each teacher has ⁴u............................ a lot of useful ⁵l............................ for their subject. There's also an ⁶a............................ for your phone, which you can ⁷d............................ from the website. There's nothing to ⁸i............................ – it's easy!

READING

1 Imagine that you're at your friend's house and your phone rings. It's Mum. And it's the fourth time she's called. Tick (✔) what you would do.

Pick up the phone immediately – it might be important. ☐
Let it ring – you've already sent her a text. ☐
Turn your phone to 'silent'. You don't want another call! ☐
Something else (say what). ☐

....

2 Read the text. What did Bradley's mum do when he didn't answer his phone?

....

Pick up the phone!

Do you always answer the phone when your mum calls, or do you ignore it?

You may not be able to do that for much longer. A mother from Houston, USA, Sharon Standifird, was annoyed because she was unable to get her teenagers to answer the phone. So she did a search online. She didn't know much about app development but, with some help, she created the app. It's on sale and it's called 'Ignore No More'.

What does the app do? If you don't answer your mum's call, the phone locks. This means that you can't go onto Facebook, or play games, or text, or call anyone else. The only thing you can do is call your mum. However, the app allows you to make an emergency phone call.

All your mum or dad has to do is to find your number on their phone, then they type in a password and your phone is 'blocked' – it doesn't work. You have to call your mum. So what did her son, Bradley, think? He thought the app was a good idea, but he didn't like the idea that his mum would use it for him!

What do you think? Good idea?

Comments

Zara   I think it's a really good idea. There are kids in my class that never call their parents. It's not right – I mean, they just want to know that you are safe. It's not difficult.

Kyle   Pretty creative Mum! I hope mine doesn't learn about it! But seriously if your mum calls, you should always pick up the phone. Usually they just want to know that you are OK. No big deal! ☺

Darcie   How embarrassing! That would definitely make me answer the phone! But you know, sometimes you are in an area where the phone really doesn't work. ☺

3 Read the text again. Are these sentences true (T) or false (F)?

1 Sharon created the app on her own. ....
2 The app is free to all parents. ....
3 If you do not answer your mum's call or text, you will still be able to call the police. ....
4 Your mum or dad creates a special password. ....
5 Sharon's son, Bradley, wanted his mum to create the app for him. ....
6 Zara agrees with the app and its use. ....
7 Kyle thinks it might not always be a good time to answer the phone. ....
8 Darcie says that in some areas the phone might not ring. ....

4 Match the highlighted words in the text to their meanings.

1 a dangerous situation which requires help immediately   ....
2 available to buy in a shop or online   ....
3 work that is done to create something new   ....
4 gives permission   ....
5 answer the phone   ....

EP Word profile *turn*

Complete the sentences with the correct form of *turn*.

1 Can you .... the music .... please? It's too loud.
2 .... the TV now. It's time for our game show!
3 If you .... right at the roundabout, the café is on the left.
4 She .... to the last page to read the ending.
5 It's our .... to go first.

GRAMMAR   Present simple passive

1 Complete the sentences with the correct form of the present simple passive.

1 The phone .... , so the child has to call an adult. (lock)

2 Many apps .... with new phones. (give away)

3 Computer games .... by programmers. (write)

4 English .... in many countries. (speak)

5 In tourist places, many photos .... (take).

6 Not much .... about the latest computer virus. (know)

7 Mum .... every day by an annoying advertising company. (phone)

8 Children .... by their teachers at school. (help)

2 Rewrite these sentence using the present simple passive.

1 People take orders at the bar.

   ....

2 They offer several types of fruit juice on the menu.

   ....

3 They use real fruit.

   ....

4 They make the drinks in the kitchen behind the café.

   ....

5 They bring the drinks to your table.

   ....

6 The waiters wear uniforms.

   ....

7 They close the café on Sundays.

   ....

3 Complete the text with the present simple passive form of the words in the box, as in the example. There is one negative.

> create   delete   design   ~~enjoy~~   intend
> see   store   share   use   watch

Many social media sites ¹ _are enjoyed_ by teens and ² _i_........................... to give you a different experience. Snapchat ³ _d_........................... to let you share fun videos and photos just for a moment because, after a short time, the picture disappears. But Snapchat pictures and videos ⁴ _d_........................... because data lasts for ever and so it ⁵ _s_........................... somewhere on the internet.

Photos and text ⁶ _s_........................... on tumblr. When you sign up, a password ⁷ _c_........................... and these sites ⁸ _u_........................... for personal photos and information.

Short videos ⁹ _w_........................... on Vine. Some are funny, others aren't! If you don't change the settings, everything ¹⁰ _s_........................... by everyone.

4 ⊙ Correct the mistakes in these sentences or tick (✔) any you think are correct.

1 My best friend is call Sean.

   ....

2 You are invite to the picnic next Saturday at the park.

   ....

3 It will be hold in Tao Dan Park.

   ....

4 The game can be played by two players.

   ....

5 She called Michelle.

   ....

VOCABULARY   Phrasal verbs: technology

1 **Match the phrasal verbs to their meanings.**

1	look up	....	**a**	reduce the level of sound or heat that something produces
2	put in	....	**b**	remove something from somewhere
3	switch on / turn on	....	**c**	change a channel on a TV
4	turn up	....	**d**	find a piece of information in a book or on a computer
5	take out	....	**e**	increase the level of sound or heat that a machine produces
6	turn over / switch over	....	**f**	make an electric light, TV, etc. start working
7	switch off / turn off	....	**g**	place something inside something else
8	turn down	....	**h**	stop an electric light, TV, etc. working

2 **Complete the sentences with the words in the box.**

> down   off   off   out   on   up

1 Before she goes to bed, Mum turns .... the TV.
2 It's easy to look .... information on the computer.
3 It was too hot and so I turned the heating ....
4 When you're in the theatre you have to switch .... your phone.
5 Have you switched .... the computer yet? I need it now.
6 Dad and Nathan took the battery .... of the car.

WRITING   Notes and messages

See Prepare to write box, Student's Book page 79.

1 **Read Bill's note. Which question is he answering, a or b?**

Hi Sam,

Sorry about losing your book. When I got off the bus, I realised I didn't have it with me. Do you want to meet at the bookshop on Saturday to choose a new one?

See you soon!

Bill

ⓐ

You have lost a book that belonged to your friend, Sam. Write him a note. In your note, you should
• apologise
• say what happened
• invite him to choose a new one.

ⓑ

You gave your friend Sam a book as a present, but he already had it. Write him a note. In your note, you should
• invite Sam to go with you to choose another book
• suggest when you could both do this
• remind Sam to bring the book so that you can exchange it.

2 **Complete these notes and messages with the words in the box.**

> could you   thanks a lot   do you want to
> remember to   sorry about   good luck!

Hi Lucy, Here are the DVDs. ¹............................. take them back before 6 pm!

Dad, Please ²............................. look in the car and see if I left my phone there? I can't find it.

Hi Ben, I have to go shopping on Saturday and look for a present for Mum for Mother's Day.
³............................. come with me?

Hi Mum, ⁴............................. breaking the plate.
It fell out of my hands.
See you later,
Dave xx

Hope everything goes well this afternoon! Stay calm and ⁵............................. ! Love Jill.

Hi Dad,
⁶............................. for the money for the cinema!
It was really kind!

3 **Write your answer to the question that Bill didn't answer from exercise 1.**

• Write 35–45 words.
• Remember to check your spelling and grammar.

16 Wish me luck!

VOCABULARY   Verb + noun

1 Match the verbs to their meanings.

1 blow out ....
2 give ....
3 pour ....
4 spill ....
5 break ....
6 cross (your fingers) ....
7 touch ....
8 step ....
9 pull out ....

a put one over another
b lift your foot and put it down in a different place
c separate into two or more pieces
d provide someone with something, often as a present
e stop a candle from burning by blowing on it
f make something fall from a container without meaning to
g put your hand on something
h take hold of something and remove it
i make a liquid flow into or out of a container

2 Choose the correct verb to complete the phrase.

> blow out   give   pour   spill   break
> cross   touch   step   pull out

1 .... on gaps in the pavement
2 .... salt
3 .... wood
4 .... a mirror
5 .... your fingers
6 .... grey hair
7 .... coffee
8 .... candles
9 .... a bunch of flowers

3 Choose the correct verb.

1 Max *gave / crossed* me a bunch of flowers.
2 *Blow out / Touch* the candles and make a wish!
3 I think I did well in that exam – *touch / pull out* wood.
4 If you *break / touch* that mirror, you'll get seven years' bad luck.
5 I don't think it's a good idea to *pull out / break* grey hairs.
6 Kevin doesn't like *stepping / pouring* on the gaps in the pavement.
7 Mum's *pouring / spilling* coffee for everyone.
8 As the teacher told us our results, I *crossed / touched* my fingers.
9 Bia *spilled / gave* salt on the table.

4 Complete the text with the words and phrases in the box.

> the candles   bunch of flowers   coffee
> the salt   your shoulder   wood

Yesterday it was Abigail's birthday dinner and the theme was 'lucky!' I gave her a [1] .... Then we had dinner and during the main course Abigail suddenly yelled 'Oh no! I've spilt [2] .... '. So, of course, if you do that, you have to throw some of it over [3] .... for good luck. Then her mum brought in a cake and she blew out [4] .... and made a wish. After dinner, her mum poured [5] .... , and we talked about our plans. Mac said, 'I want to get good exam results' – touching [6] .... as he put his hand on the table.

READING

1 Read the article about Feng Shui and add the correct headings (a–g) to the paragraphs (1–6). There is one heading you don't need.

a Decoration
b Put the furniture back
c Fresh and clean
d North or south?
e Wind and water
f What is Feng Shui?
g Tidy up

2 Read the article again. Are these sentences true (T) or false (F)?

1 Feng Shui can help you pass your exams. ....
2 You need to put all your things on the floor first. ....
3 Knowing the direction your room faces is necessary. ....
4 Washing your windows brings bad luck. ....
5 You should place your bed under a window. ....
6 It's better to avoid having plants in your bedroom. ....

Exams coming up? Problems with friends? Not feeling too good? It seems that Feng Shui could be the answer. Read on!

1 ....

If you look online, you'll see there are many answers to that question. But, simply put, Feng Shui is about balance: the right amount of energy in the right places. Feng means 'wind' and shui means 'water'. In Chinese culture these are linked to good health. If you're in good health, you'll feel good. If you feel good, your life will be better.

2 ....

First, you need to clear up by putting everything in the right place, including all of last year's books that are still under the bed and anything else that's in the way. Everything has a place – you just need to find it! It's really important to throw away the rubbish in your room – check your drawers, your wardrobe and, of course, under the bed!
Once you've done that, then you can start the fun part: Feng Shui.

3 ....

Get a compass to find out where north, south, east and west are in your room. If your phone hasn't already got one, you can download an app. Then stand in the middle of the room and check the direction of north. Make a drawing of your room and divide it into nine squares. Write the direction – N for north, and so on – in each square.

4 ....

You need to get out the vacuum cleaner and clean the floor, clear the dust, and wash your windows, and ceiling fans if you have them. Choose cleaning products with your favourite smell.

5 ....

So now, where should you put your furniture? There are a few things to remember here. Don't put your bed with your feet facing the door, and try to have a wall behind your bed, not a window. Place your study desk in the north-east corner of your room.

6 ....

If you place a lamp in the north-east corner, it will bring you luck in education and if you put it in the south-west corner, it will bring you luck in friendship. Maybe you need two lamps! Choose pictures that make you happy. If you have a noticeboard, then hang it on the south wall. If you have certificates for anything, then put them here too. And for extra energy, paint a wall red!

Plants are not a good idea for your bedroom as they use up body energy, and ceiling fans are not a good idea either because they move energy around. However, if you live in a hot country, then you need them.

All in all, if your environment is calm, you will be more comfortable and achieve more.

---

3 Match the highlighted words in the text to their meanings.

1 things that you throw away because you don't want them ....

2 the power that comes from something like water or wind ....

3 powder from tiny pieces of dirt that you can see on surfaces such as tables or in the air. ....

4 documents that give details to show that something is true ....

5 a board on the wall where you put advertisements and announcements ....

6 something you use to find out where north, south, east and west are ....

EP Word profile *luck*

Match the sentence halves and add the correct form of *luck*.

1 Why are you wearing that hat? ....
2 Why are you crying? ....
3 Did our team win the match? ....
4 How did you get home? ....
5 That's nice – is it new? ....
6 How did you get onto the football team? ....
7 Did you remember to bring the game? ....
8 Do you like black cats? ....

a No! They are .... in my country!
b I have no idea. .... , I guess!
c I've lost my .... pencil.
d It brings me good .... !
e Yes! It's a .... stone. I got it yesterday.
f Yes, ... Mum reminded me!
g No, they were............................ . They missed a goal opportunity.
h .... , I had some money for the bus ticket.

GRAMMAR   Zero and first conditional

1 Complete the zero conditional sentences using the correct form of the verbs in brackets in the correct order.

1 If you .... your lucky number, you .... happy. (feel, see)

2 If you .... water, it .... at 100 °C. (boil, heat)

3 I .... always exhausted the next day if I .... to bed very late. (be, go)

4 They .... the schools in America if the temperature .... to -20 °C. (close, drop)

5 If my sister .... under a ladder, she .... she will have bad luck. (think, walk)

6 My brother .... better if he .... exercise in the morning. (do, feel)

2 Complete the text with the correct form of the verbs in the box.

| become   pour   get   go   make   say |

There is a hole in my roof. When it rains, the water
¹............................. in. When the water comes in, it
²............................. the floor wet. When the floor is
wet, the walls ³............................. green. When the
walls are green, I ⁴............................. ill. When I am
ill, I ⁵............................. to the doctor. When I see the
doctor, he always ⁶............................. the same thing:
'Fix the roof!'

3 Match the sentence halves.

1 If you catch the bunch of flowers at a wedding, ...

2 If you catch a falling leaf in autumn, ...

3 If you put new shoes on the table, ...

4 If there is a full moon, ...

5 If you eat an apple every day, ...

a it will bring you good luck.

b strange things will happen.

c you will be the next to get married.

d you will stay healthy.

e they will bring you bad luck.

4 Complete the text with the correct tense of the verbs in brackets.

My Mum's friend believes in these sayings about luck. She says that she ¹*gives / doesn't give* anyone knives as a present because they ²*cut / don't cut* your friendship. If there ³*is / will be* a party on Friday 13th, she ⁴*don't go / won't go*. Last week she was very unhappy because her daughter put her new shoes on the table. If you ⁵*do / will do* that, you ⁶*has / will have* a lot of bad luck. It ⁷*isn't / won't be* a good thing to live your life like this unless you ⁸*know / will know* it's true. But last week our teacher gave our test results back and I didn't get a good result. Maybe it's true that if a black cat ⁹*crosses / will cross* your path, you ¹⁰*won't have / will have* bad luck. That's what happened to me before the test!

5 ⊙ Choose the correct sentence in each pair.

1 a If you'll meet her, I'm sure that you'll like her.
   b If you meet her, I'm sure that you'll like her.

2 a If you don't go with us, you'll missed out on a lot of fun.
   b If you don't go with us, you'll miss out on a lot of fun.

3 a If you go, it will be better than it was.
   b If you will go, it will be better than it was.

4 a It'll be a pleasure if you came.
   b It'll be a pleasure if you come.

5 a I was a little scared of her because if she doesn't smile then she looks like an angry person.
   b I was a little scared of her because if she doesn't smile then she will look like an angry person.

VOCABULARY   *if* and *unless*

1 Choose the correct word to complete the sentences.

1 *If / Unless* you finish your homework, you won't go to the party later.

2 I'll pick you up at 4 pm *unless / if* you call me earlier.

3 You'll have to pay a fine *if / unless* you don't return the library book.

4 *If / Unless* you order a fresh fruit juice, you'll have to wait for them to make it.

5 You won't get a ticket *if / unless* you buy one online today.

6 Freddie will check your homework *if / unless* you want him to.

7 We won't sleep in a tent *if / unless* the rain stops.

8 Maggie will download the music for you *if / unless* her Dad helps her.

9 *If / Unless* you practise hard, you will be very lucky!

10 I won't ask Mum to help me with my homework *if / unless* I can't do it by myself.

2 Rewrite the sentences so that the second sentence means the same as the first.

1 If you go now, you'll get to the shops before they close.
Unless you go now, ... the shops before they close.

2 You won't be able to do the test unless you get the notes from Max.
If you get the notes from Max, ... do the test.

3 If you aren't quiet, you won't be able to work in the library.
You .... unless you're quiet.

4 We'll arrive at 12.00 unless the bus is late.
If the bus is late, ... at 12.00.

5 I'll get dinner ready for 6 pm if you don't call me before.
I'll get dinner ready for 6 pm unless ....

6 Unless we get more members, the youth club won't stay open.
If .... , the youth club will stay open.

LISTENING

1 Look at the photos. Which of the descriptions do you think is not correct?

These may …
1 bring you luck.
2 show you bad people.
3 keep you healthy.
4 make you happy.
5 keep away bad luck.

2 ▶14 Listen to the first part of a conversation between a boy, Aran, and a girl, Michelle, about things you can wear for luck. Complete the missing words.

Aran: That was an interesting [1]............................ , wasn't it, Michelle?

Michelle: Yes, if you believe what they said. I mean, how can holding a [2]............................ really make you better? I don't think that's likely at all!

Aran: But there are a lot of people who believe in the [3]............................ of objects, like special stones from the [4]............................ . So why did you buy that [5]............................ and red one then? I mean, it's beautiful, of course, but …

3 ▶15 Now listen to the full conversation and answer the questions.

1 What did Michelle buy?
....

2 Why did she buy it (two reasons)?
....
....

3 Why does Aran think some people wear necklaces?
....

4 Where did Michelle buy a necklace?
....

5 What did Aran say his ring helped him to finish?
....

6 What were the 'lucky eyes' that people used to have?
....

4 ▶15 Listen again. Are the sentences correct (C) or incorrect (I)?

1 Michelle believes that certain objects have special power. ....

2 Aran and Michelle agree that the stone she bought is attractive. ....

3 Michelle is being serious when she tells Aran about the necklace. ....

4 Aran believes that a piece of jewellery brought him luck recently. ....

5 Aran says that in the past there were more lucky objects than today. ....

6 Aran thinks that Michelle might change her mind about her lucky stone. ....

VOCABULARY Creative lives: nouns

1 Complete the crossword, using the clues below.

Across

2 a picture made with a pencil or pen
5 a film company or a place where films are made
7 a book that tells a story about imaginary people and events
9 a piece of art that is made from stone, wood, clay, etc.
10 the life story of a person written by someone else

Down

1 someone who writes books, or the words for a film
3 the people who sit and watch a performance at a theatre
4 someone who creates pictures
6 someone who writes poems
8 a room or building which is used for showing works of art

2 Write the letters in the correct order to make words connected with talent.

1 NILGMIF ....
2 CREDORIT ....
3 THIBINEXOI ....
4 TAPNIGIN ....
5 TRYPEO ....
6 TRIPCS ....
7 EIRESS ....
8 TREWIR ....

3 Underline the odd one out, as in the example.

0	painting	poetry	sculpture	<u>audience</u>
1	novel	script	poet	biography
2	exhibition	gallery	studio	novel
3	filming	director	script	studio
4	poet	painter	writer	sculpture
5	drawings	paintings	sculpture	writer
6	director	writer	audience	painter

4 Complete the text with the words in the box. There is one word you don't need.

> drawings   exhibition   gallery   painter
> paintings   poet   poetry   sculpture   series

Last week I went to an [1] .... called 'Chickens'. It was held in the local art [2] .... and it showed the work of the local [3] ...., Katija Vorelli, amongst others. As we arrived, we saw an enormous [4] .... of a chicken outside the building! Then we went inside. Katija usually only does colourful [5] .... but this time she included some pencil [6] .... The [7] ...., Ricardo Peters, was also there and he read some of his [8] .... It was a fun evening and gave me some ideas for my own paintings and drawings.

READING

1 Read the article quickly and complete the sentence below.

This article was probably written for
1 a classical music magazine.
2 a teen magazine.
3 a weekly newspaper.

2 Read the article again. Decide if each sentence is correct (C) or incorrect (I).

1 The singer uses part of her real name as her stage name. ....
2 The singer's mother is famous for writing poetry. ....
3 A school event was important for her career. ....
4 She was given a Grammy for singing something on her own. ....
5 She was upset that a fan wanted to do a project about her. ....
6 Although she is still a teenager, she is confident when she is with adults. ....

Every month we feature a different artist. Here is a young
New Zealander who has already made a big name for herself.

Bio

Ella Marija Lani Yelich-O'Connor is a young teen singer-songwriter. You may recognise her stage name, Lorde. The daughter of a well-known female poet, she grew up in Auckland. At the age of 12, someone from a music company saw her in a school talent show and because of this, she was offered a recording contract with Universal Music New Zealand.

Success

She became the first female artist in 17 years to get to the top of the song chart, and in 2014 she won two Grammy awards. One was for the best song of the year, Royals, and the other was for the best individual performance. Her name was suggested for many more prizes.

So young

Social media is an obvious way to stay in touch with your fans, and there are many websites about Lorde, as well as blogs written by fans. One of her followers told her that she wanted to do lots of school projects about her. The artist replied saying she really liked doing school projects and she loved the idea that someone wanted to do one on her. By reading her comments and posts, it's easy to see why young people love her. She is young herself and teens like her as she sings about teen-related issues. And so far, she seems to be able to handle working in the real world with people who are much older than she is.

Future?

As she grows older, will she continue to be popular with a teen audience? Or will she and they grow old together?

What do you think?

She's just the best. If she carries on like this, she'll do really well. Go Lorde!
@rainbows

There are so many young singers who are great for one album but that's it. She seems really nice though and deserves success. Good luck!:)
@love34

I don't know. She's got a great voice but that's all. People will get bored of her and someone else will appear. Musicians these days aren't like the old greats.
@flea_pea02

Hide comments ▲

---

3 **Match the highlighted words in the text to their meanings.**

1 acting, dancing singing, or playing music to entertain people ....

2 when two people or companies agree to work together and sign a document ....

3 several songs or pieces of music on a CD or download ....

4 people who perform songs, often as a job ....

5 someone who paints, draws, makes sculptures or sings ....

6 websites where you write your own thoughts and change them regularly ....

EP Word profile *own*

Complete the sentences with *own* **and any other words you need.**

1 Has everyone got their .... pen?

2 Jessica completed that drawing .... – amazing because she's only three years old!

3 I thought you had a bag ....

4 My brother's a painter – he likes working .... in his studio.

5 Our neighbours .... a boat.

GRAMMAR   Reported commands

1 Add the missing vowels (A, E, I, O, U) to make reporting verbs.

1 W .... RN ....

2 .... SK ....

3 .... RD .... R ....

4 T .... LL ....

5 .... DV .... S ....

6 P .... RS .... D ....

7 R .... M .... ND ....

8 C .... NV .... NC ....

2 Write the words in the correct order to make sentences.

1 near / us / warned / not / He / the water / to go

....

2 explain / We / the artist's ideas / the teacher / asked / to

....

3 ordered / The / us / be / headteacher / quiet / to

....

4 me / Billy / my / eyes / to / not / open / told

....

5 with / advised / again / to / not / me / her / Lorraine / argue

....

6 persuaded / Felix / to / buy / the latest PlayStation / his parents

....

7 us / Dad / the school trip / to / give / the details / reminded / about / him

....

8 me / to / the school film night / Mum / convinced / go / to

....

3 Complete the comments. Use the reporting verbs in brackets and add any other words you need.

1 'You should go round the exhibition together', said the man.
The man .... round the exhibition together. (advise)

2 'Show me your tickets, please,' said the security man.
The security man .... our tickets. (ask)

3 'Wait at the door!' he said.
He .... at the door. (order)

4 'You mustn't walk there!' said the woman.
The woman .... there. (warn)

5 'Remove all phones from your bags, please.'
He .... all our phones from our bags. (tell)

6 'Let's go to the café first!' said Kari.
Kari .... to the café first. (persuade)

7 Don't forget to text your mum.
My brother .... my mum. (remind)

8 'Don't buy the pink dress.'
She .... the pink dress. (convince)

4 Complete the report of the conversation with the correct form of the reporting verbs in box A and the verbs in box B.

A ask   persuade   remind   tell

B add   go   help   not get

Mum: Lili, help me with dinner, please.

Lili: Sure. Remember Josh is coming for dinner, so add some extra meat for him!

Mum: Yeah, sure. Do you think you could go to the shops to get some more for me?

Lili: Oh, Mum, really?

Mum: Well, I also want to make a pudding and there isn't any chocolate.

Lili: I'm going now!

Mum: Don't get milk chocolate, please – I need dark.

Mum [1] .... Lili [2] .... her with dinner. Lili [3] .... Mum [4] .... more meat for Josh. Mum [5] .... Lili [6] .... to the shops for her. Mum [7] .... Lili [8] .... milk chocolate because she needed dark chocolate.

5 ⊙ Correct the mistakes in these sentences or tick (✔) any you think are correct.

1 She said to me to look through the window and see the weather.

....

2 I opened it and read the letter which told to give back the money.

....

3 We were in the same class and the teacher asked for us to do a project together.

....

4 We were both playing football at the club, and the trainer told us to play together.

....

5 We were talking and a boy in front of us tell us be quiet.

....

VOCABULARY   Adjectives: -al and -ful

1 Make adjectives from these nouns. Use -al or -ful.

1 help   ....

2 nature   ....

3 environment ....

4 profession ....

5 peace   ....

6 stress   ....

7 pain   ....

8 culture   ....

9 politics   ....

10 music   ....

11 success   ....

12 tradition ....

2 Complete the film reviews with the correct form of the words in brackets.

I loved this ¹........................... (origin) film! It showed the ²........................... (colour) landscape of Africa. There was nothing ³........................... (politics) – it just was a ⁴........................... (peace) film about people living their lives.

This is not a ⁵........................... (cheer) film. It's about a footballer who has a bad accident and his ⁶........................... (pain) recovery. However, the acting was ⁷........................... (profession) and ⁸........................... (nature). I think it will be a ⁹........................... (success) film.

WRITING   An informal letter

See Prepare to write box, Student's Book page 23.

1 Do you have a performing arts festival or an arts festival at your school? Tick (✔) the sentence that is right for you.

Yes, it's an annual event and I love it!   ☐

No, I don't think so.   ☐

Yes, but I don't take part.   ☐

No, we don't, but I wish we did.   ☐

2 Read the letter. How would Will answer exercise 1?

....

3 Complete the letter with the adjectives in the box.

amazing   excited   latest
performing   nervous   short

Hi Maxi,

I'm so ¹........................... because it's our ²........................... arts festival next week.

Every year, all the students take part in some way. You can enter a painting or drawing for the art exhibition, or you can make a ³........................... film, or you can read your poetry.

Of course, there are lots of people who do ⁴........................... musical performances.

The important thing is that as many students as possible do something.

This year my best friend and I are going to perform our ⁵........................... song. We wrote it together. I play the guitar and he sings. I'm a bit ⁶........................... but it'll be fun!

Send me your news!

Will

4 Read this part of a letter you have received from your New Zealand friend. How many questions do you have to answer?

For my homework project, I have to write about an interesting exhibition from your country. Which exhibition have you enjoyed recently in your country? Why did you decide to go there? What things did you especially like about it?

5 Make notes to answer the questions in the letter. Add some adjectives you can use.

....

....

....

....

6 Write your letter to your friend.

- Use your notes to help you.
- Write about 100 words.
- Remember to check your spelling and grammar.

VOCABULARY   Work

1 **Complete the puzzle using the clues below, then find the hidden word. Which person …**

1 plays music on the radio or at live events?
2 teaches people to improve at a sport?
3 plays a musical instrument?
4 writes books, articles, plays, blogs, etc.?
5 repairs the engines of vehicles and other machines?
6 gives you advice about the law?
7 tells the people in a film what to do? (two words)
8 stops fires from burning?
9 studies and works in science?
10 gives medical care to animals that are ill or hurt?

Hidden word: ....

2 **Read what these teens want to do. Choose a suitable job for them.**

1 ....

I want to work with people and I'd like to help them. I like working in a team and I don't mind being in dangerous situations.

2 ....

I want to do a job where I can write. I love writing and giving opinions. But I don't want to be sitting at a desk all day. I want to be with people and ask them questions.

3 ....

I want to create things. I'd really like to draw pictures of clothes that people can wear, and then try to make them. I think that would be awesome.

4 ....

I want to solve crimes – just like on TV! Get the bad guys!

7 ....

I like being outside. I'm quite strong and I don't mind lifting heavy weights. I'd like to do a job where I'm helping to make something useful and perhaps beautiful.

5 ....

I don't really know what I want to do. But I think while I'm at university, I'll get a part-time job working with children. I think that would be good.

6 ....

My friend wants to show off clothes. She loves it when people take photographs of her.

3 **Underline the odd one out.**

1 You might work with children in this job.
   babysitter   mechanic   coach   musician
2 You write a lot in these jobs.
   journalist   author   scientist   babysitter
3 These jobs can be hard and you must be fit.
   vet   firefighter   builder   author
4 You can do these jobs on your own.
   firefighter   detective   author   musician
5 You have to be creative for these jobs.
   designer   vet   journalist   author
6 You tell people what to do in these jobs.
   film director   coach   model   babysitter
7 You have to study for many years to do these jobs.
   lawyer   vet   DJ   scientist

READING

1 **Read the article quickly. Who is it for – parents or teens?**

....

2 **Tick (✔) the best title for the article.**

1 Help your mum and dad ☐
2 What do you think about pocket money? ☐
3 How do you spend your money? ☐

3 **Read the article again and complete these sentences.**

1 The magazine asked .... and their parents what they thought about pocket money.

2 Some teens receive money every ....

3 Some teens have to .... in the house to earn their money.

4 Teens generally .... their money on fun things.

5 Many teens are .... up for expensive items.

6 Some of the teens were interested in .... more money.

7 Most teens don't like asking their parents to .... them more money.

4 **Who said this – a parent or a teen?**

1 ....

> I have to think carefully about money. It's important that Kerry has her own money but she has to understand the value of it. But generally she doesn't ask for silly things.

2 ....

> I'm lucky – my parents are teaching me about money. If I need more money, they lend it to me, but I have to pay it back. But it's not a good idea to spend if it isn't really yours. I did that once but not any more. Now I save. I think I learnt a good lesson!

3 ....

> I get the same amount every week. In the holidays I usually get a bit more. Then for my birthday I usually get money too. Some of my classmates get a lot more than I do.

4 ....

> I don't give Pepe any money. If he wants something, or some money, he asks me. If I think it's reasonable, I give it to him. My parents did the same with me.

5 **Match the highlighted words in the text to their meanings.**

1 money on your mobile phone ....

2 be able to buy something because you have enough money ....

3 willing to give ....

4 wanting to know or learn about something ....

5 happening often, especially at the same time every day or week, etc. ....

6 not taking help or money from other people ....

We asked you and your parents what you thought about pocket money. We wanted to know if you have enough money to do the things you want to. We were also curious to find out if your parents thought they were giving you too much and whether any of you had to do jobs to 'earn' your pocket money.

What the parents say

Some parents give their teens money at regular times, for example, weekly. This is often increased by gifts from grandparents and other generous family members. Many parents thought that their children should do something for the money and so quite a few of you out there do jobs around the home, such as cleaning and helping out in the garden. But some parents think that their children should do that kind of thing anyway and so shouldn't be paid. Many parents wanted to give their teens more but said it was difficult to afford it.

What you say

Most of you receive some pocket money either every week or month but some of you are only given money when you need it. You spend it on being with your friends, food, clothes and make up, and music. One 15-year-old was also paying for his mobile phone credit. Lots of you help your parents out when they are busy and we think that's a great attitude. There were also a lot of you who were saving up for things like a tablet or better phone, and you were looking for ways to earn more money. But most of you don't want to ask for money because you want to be independent.

EP **Word profile** *go*

Match the sentence halves.

1 Jonas and his Dad are	....	**a**	on – there was so much noise.
2 Uncle Frank went	....	**b**	on till 7 pm last night.
3 I can't find Zac anywhere.	....	**c**	away! He was mad at me.
4 Tomorrow at the beach, I want to have	....	**d**	grey in his 30s.
5 My brother told me to go	....	**e**	a go at surfing.
6 Are we going	....	**f**	away on holiday this year?
7 Football practice went	....	**g**	going to France by plane.
8 Our teacher asked what was going	....	**h**	I can't either. I think he's gone.

GRAMMAR   Second conditional

1 **Match the sentence halves.**

1 I'd buy a new mobile phone ....
2 If you could visit South America, ...
3 How would you feel if ....
4 If you didn't talk so much, ...
5 If you apologised, ...
6 If you looked more carefully, ...
7 Would you feel better ....

a you would hear everything the teacher said.
b I would forgive you.
c if you sat down?
d which country would you choose?
e you would find your pen.
f you lost your new sunglasses?
g if I had enough money.

2 **Complete the second conditional sentences with the correct form of the verbs in brackets.**

1 I .... the bus here, if I .... you. (not catch, be)
2 If you .... more exercise, you .... better. (do, feel)
3 I .... her to my account if I .... her Instagram name, (add, know)
4 If she .... an umbrella, she .... wet. (have, get)
5 Bob .... his family on holiday if he .... the lottery. (take, win)
6 I .... on the school trip if I .... so ill, (go, not feel)
7 If I .... a famous person, I .... them lots of questions! (meet, ask)
8 .... to the music festival if I .... you a ticket? (go, give)

3 **Complete the text with the correct form of the verbs in the box.**

become	become	do	go	get
happen	practise	see	study	study

?

People often ask what I want to do in the future.
If I [1]............................ into the future, what
[2]............................? If I [3]............................
harder, I [4]............................ better marks. If
that [5]............................ , I [6]............................
university to study law. If I [7]............................ law,
I [8]............................ a lawyer. But I don't want to!
I want to be a musician! I love playing the guitar but if
I [9]............................ every day, [10]............................ a
famous musician? I wish I could see into the future!

4 **Rewrite the sentences using the second conditional.**

1 It's raining so we can't go to the beach.
   If it .... , we ....
2 I haven't got a bike and so I can't cycle to your house.
   If I .... , I ....
3 I can't buy that video game because I haven't got any money .
   If I .... , I ....
4 The film is on too late, so I'm not going to watch it.
   If the film .... , I ....
5 We don't buy that ice cream because it is expensive.
   If that ice cream .... , we ....

5 ⊙ **Choose the correct sentence in each pair.**

1 a Mum promised the children she would buy some sweets for them.
   b Mum promised the children she will bought some sweets for them.
2 a She would leave anything she was doing if I needed her to.
   b She would leave anything she was doing if I need her to.
3 a My parents would be very happy if you accept.
   b My parents would be very happy if you accepted.
4 a I think if you met him you would like him.
   b I think if you met him you will like him.
5 a Then I remembered if I don't find it they would not let me take the class.
   b Then I remembered if I didn't find it they would not let me take the class.

VOCABULARY   Suffixes: -er, -or, -ist, -ian

1 **Make nouns for people from these words.**

1 teach......
2 build......
3 journal......
4 direct......
5 blog......
6 run......
7 support......
8 reception......
9 guitar......
10 novel......
11 act......
12 music......

2 **What do you call someone who ...**

1 works in a hotel reception? ....
2 enjoys running? ....
3 visits a place? ....
4 doesn't eat meat ....
5 cleans? ....
6 creates art for a job? ....

LISTENING

1 ▶16 **Listen to five short conversations. Decide who is speaking.**

1 **a** teacher and student   **b** teacher and parents
2 **a** aunt and nephew   **b** father and daughter
3 **a** teacher and student   **b** teen boy and boss
4 **a** teen friends   **b** parents
5 **a** girl and teacher   **b** uncle and niece

2 ▶16 **Listen again and choose the correct picture, A, B or C for each conversation.**

1 Where is the careers talk?

  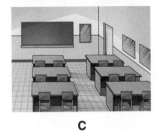

A   B   C

2 Which work experience job does the girl want to do?

  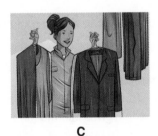

A   B   C

3 What time does the boy usually start work on Saturdays?

A   B   C

4 What did the boy do for his extra pocket money?

 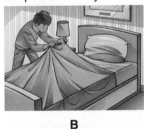 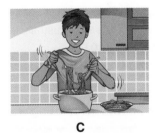

A   B   C

5 What does the girl want to do when she finishes school?

A   B   C

19 The written word

VOCABULARY   Magazines

1 Label the pictures with the correct parts of a magazine.

1 ....

3 ....

4 ....

7 ....

9 ....

2 ....

5 ....

6 ....

8 ....

10 ....

2 Match the words from exercise 1 to their meanings.

1 a part of a text that begins on a new line and usually contains several sentences   ....

2 a picture or text which tries to persuade people to buy a product or service   ....

3 the name of a book, movie, story   ....

4 the part of a story that is printed in large letters above the article   ....

5 the part of the magazine that gives information about what is inside it   ....

6 the page in a magazine where readers can write their thoughts and ideas   ....

7 a meeting between two people in which someone answers questions about themselves.   ....

8 a piece of writing on a particular subject   ....

9 the end of the magazine, often with an advert   ....

3 Complete the sentences with the correct words from exercise 1.

1 Have you read this *i*........................... with the lead singer of your favourite band?

2 Mum has written something for the *l*........................... *p*........................... of our local newspaper.

3 When I see *a*........................... for clothes like that, I want to buy them.

4 Her picture is on the *f*........................... *c*........................... of several magazines.

5 There's an interesting *a*........................... about sport in history.

6 The *h*........................... was 'Rain Cancels Festival'.

7 In the first *p*........................... the writer usually tells you what they are going to write about.

8 You should write no more than 10 *l*........................... .

9 There's some information about a book on the *b*........................... *c*........................... of this magazine.

10 What's the *t*........................... of your story?

4 Complete the conversation with the missing words. There is one you don't need.

> articles   advert   back cover   front cover   interview   letters page   line   title

A: Have you seen this new magazine? It looks really good and it's full of interesting [1]........................... .

B: Yes, I really like the [2]........................... . There isn't a model but they have photos of places taken by the readers.

A: Hmm, but if you read the [3]........................... , a lot of people don't like that. And they don't like the [4]........................... design either, with more readers' photos – of their food this time. And then there's information from the company. It's really an [5]........................... – but they just don't pay for it.

B: Hmm, I see what you mean. But the writing is great. Did you read the [6]........................... with Molly Bell? Really good!

A: Yes! I agree, and on the next page there was something about how to choose the right [7]........................... for your short story. Useful for school, huh?

B: I know!

READING

1 Tick (✔) the things you like reading about on blogs.

video games	☐	homework	☐
recipes	☐	travel	☐
photos	☐	book/blog reviews	☐

2 Read the description of Tess in exercise 3 and answer the questions.

1 What does she like doing?

....

2 What does she want to learn?

....

3 What three things must the blog have?

....

3 Now read about the other teens below and <u>underline</u> the three things that they want.

1 Tess enjoys taking photographs of different things. She wants to learn more ways of doing this and would like to find out about new equipment. She hopes to discover similar blogs too.

2 Adam already follows blogs about sport and is looking for one that is different. He loves giving his opinions on a range of different subjects and enjoys reading what other people think.

3 Bryony loves finding out about life outside the city and especially anything about nature. Her other main interest is cooking and she would like some ideas for dishes using fresh food.

4 Ben is looking for information about good novels to read. He is mainly interested in new ones, but also some classics. He wants a blog that will accept his own reviews.

4 The teenagers are all looking for a new blog to follow. Read the six descriptions of blogs (A–F) below. Decide which blog would be the most suitable for each teen in exercise 3.

1 Tess ......
2 Adam ......
3 Bryony ......
4 Ben ......

A ▶ Daisychain.blog

This is an unusual blog. The blogger sets a question for readers to answer on their own blogs. It's called a 'blog chain'. Each blogger then tells Daisychain when they can post, and Daisychain makes a timetable. So each day readers go to a different blog to read about the current topic.

B ▶ Foodilove.blog

This is a series of photographs that the blogger has taken herself, or has taken from other sites. They all show healthy food items and the blogger obviously loves a good breakfast! You can post your own comments on the blog and find links to other blogs about cooking.

C ▶ Thingstodo.blog

This is a blog for anyone who likes using a camera. Every month the blogger looks at a different topic, and puts lots of his own pictures on the site. He writes about the latest things you can buy and describes the various techniques that he uses too. There are also links to other useful sites.

D ▶ Thinkaboutit.blog

This blogger has strong opinions and writes about a different subject every month. He includes links to recent newspaper articles, but doesn't allow readers to share their own comments, which is a shame. Still, he definitely makes you think about life!

E ▶ Readon.blog

This blog has thousands of followers and readers are invited to send in their own pieces on favourite books. The blog tells you about books you can find in shops, and e-books too. A user-friendly system puts them into groups, so that you can easily find what you are looking for, from cookbooks to the latest fiction.

F ▶ Whatcanimake.blog

This is a food blog with a difference! The blogger writes about food that is available in a particular season and links this information to beautiful photographs of fields, woods and lakes. Details on what to prepare in the kitchen include old favourites like fruit cake, but also new things that the blogger has created.

EP Word profile *mean*

Match the beginnings and ends of sentences.

1	This sign means	......	a	to hurt you! Sorry!
2	What do you mean when you	......	b	say it's horrible? I like it!
3	This song means	......	c	I can easily access the internet!
4	Oh no! I didn't mean	......	d	I mean melons?
5	Having a smartphone means	......	e	a lot to me.
6	Do you like mangoes –	......	f	you must stop.

GRAMMAR   Reported speech

1 Match the direct speech (1–4) to the reported speech (a–d).

1 'I write for the blog,' she said.   ....
2 'I'm writing for the blog,' she said.   ....
3 'I'll write for the blog,' she said.   ....
4 'I can write for the blog,' she said.   ....

a She said she could write for the blog.
b She said she was writing for the blog.
c She said she wrote for the blog.
d She said she would write for the blog.

2 Rewrite these sentences using reported speech.

1 'She's cooking dinner.'
Emma said ....
2 'Mrs Jones will help me next week.'
Ben said ....
3 'I don't want to buy a new computer.'
Fatima said ....
4 'I hate reading books online.'
My brother said ....
5 'Dad can't get here on time.'
Mum said ....
6 'Matt isn't doing his homework.'
My mum said ....
7 'Jo's dad can pick us up.'
Alison said ....
8 'We won't be there.'
They said ....

3 Your Canadian cousin is on holiday. She's talking to you on the phone. What she is saying is different from what she said yesterday. Correct her!

1 Here it's cloudy.
Really? You said ....!
(sunny)
2 I'm having lunch with Uncle Albert.
Really? You said ....
(Aunty Betty)
3 I'll send you a postcard.
Really? You said ....
(email)
4 I won't get home before your birthday.
Really? You said ....
(my sister's birthday)
5 I can see the sea from my window.
Really? You said ....
(the mountains)

6 The food in the hotel isn't very tasty.
Really? You said ....
(spicy)
7 I'm not watching any TV.
Really? You said ....
(Youtube videos)
8 I can't wait to get home!
Really? You said you ....
(go away again)

4 Read these video profiles and then report what the people said.

> Hi! I'm Cassie. I'm 15 and I live in the USA. I'm studying for exams now. Then in the summer I'll go to Camp Kanosia. I love it there because I can swim and do lots of water sports.

1 Cassie said ....
....
....
....

> Hi! I'm Ian. I'm 14 and I'm from South Africa. I'm making this video profile at the moment! Next year, I'll go to a different school. It's an art school and I can study drawings, paintings and sculpture there.

2 Ian said ....
....
....
....

5 ◉ Correct the mistakes in these sentences or tick (✔) any you think are correct.

1 Jane called me, and she said that she and her brother are going to the swimming pool.
....
2 He said that he is going to the shopping centre.
....
3 I want to say you that I got a new computer game.
....
4 She saw me and she say that she knew me and we began to talk.
....
5 They said that they would go shopping and then they would watch a movie with me.
....

VOCABULARY say, speak, talk and tell

1 Complete the conversation with the correct form *say*, *speak*, *talk* or *tell*. Use some words more than once.

Paul: Hello, is that Cara?

Cara: Yes. Who's ¹............................. ?

Paul: It's Paul. I'm calling to invite you to my party on Saturday.

Cara: I'm sorry. Can you ²............................. that again? I can't hear you very well.

Paul: I ³............................. , would you like to come to my party on Saturday?

Cara: Yes, I'd love to! My cousin's here on holiday. Can she come too?

Paul: Yes, of course. ⁴............................. her she's welcome.

Cara: OK, thanks, I'll ⁵............................. her. I've got to go now. It was nice ⁶............................. to you. See you on Saturday!

2 Choose the correct word to complete the sentences.

1 Can you .... me what you mean?
   a speak   **b** tell   **c** say

2 Mum can .... four languages.
   a say   **b** talk   **c** speak

3 What did you .... ? I couldn't hear you.
   a speak   **b** talk   **c** say

4 It's always nice to .... to my best friend.
   a talk   **b** tell   **c** say

WRITING A review

See Prepare to write box, Student's Book page 111.

1 Rewrite the second sentence so it means the same as the first. Use no more than three words.

1 I've been writing blogs for 5 years and I'm 15 now.
   I've been writing blogs .... 10 years old.

2 She borrowed my computer for the afternoon.
   I .... computer for the afternoon.

3 'I love writing reviews,' she said.
   She .... writing reviews.

4 Her blogs are not very varied.
   There .... variety in her blogs.

5 The film is on really late so I don't think I'm going to watch it.
   If the film was on earlier, I .... it.

2 You see this blog post. What does the author want to know?

Ourfavouriteblog.blog

In this blog, we write reviews of blogs. There are so many blogs but this month I'd like to know about your favourite book or film blog. *Ourfavouriteblog* wants to know what information it includes, if readers can comment and why you like it.

suggest a blog

3 Read what Marielle wrote. Tick (✔) the information she includes.

1 the title of the blog ☐
2 what kind of blog it is ☐
3 how she found it ☐
4 how often it is updated ☐
5 why she likes it ☐

Ourfavouriteblog.blog

[posted at 2.39 pm]

I love reading *Ourreadingblog*. It's a blog about books for teens and it gives some really good reviews and articles. They are a good length – some blogs have very long posts. Also, *Ourreadingblog* has a few good photographs. But *Ourreadingblog* also has an Instagram and so there are photos of the covers of good books there. *Ourreadingblog* usually posts once a month but sometimes more often, when there are a lot of good books! I really like the links at the end of the review because they are useful. Readers can send in their own reviews too. It's a great blog!

[4 comments]

4 Now write about your favourite blog and why you like it.

- Write about 100 words.
- Remember to check your spelling and grammar.

20 Puzzles and tricks

VOCABULARY Puzzles

1 Match the words to their meanings.

1	puzzle	....	**a**	form an idea or picture of something in your mind
2	trick	....	**b**	something strange that cannot be explained
3	imagination	....	**c**	describes something that people cannot know about
4	hide	....	**d**	make something happen or exist
5	solve	....	**e**	describes a way of making something impossible happen
6	create	....	**f**	the ability to make pictures of something in your mind
7	mystery	....	**g**	find the answer to something by thinking about it
8	imagine	....	**h**	a game that challenges you to think a lot
9	magic (adjective)	....	**i**	put something in a place where nobody can find it
10	secret (adjective)	....	**j**	a clever activity that makes people believe something false

2 Complete the sentences with the correct words from exercise 1.

1 In our lesson, we had to .... a short play, which we performed to the class.
2 At the .... show I went to, a man made a rabbit disappear!
3 When you read books, you have to use your ....
4 My aunt does a crossword .... every day.
5 You mustn't tell anyone this .... information.
6 Can I show you my new card .... ?
7 The police are still trying to .... the crime.
8 I always .... my diary because I don't want anyone to read it.
9 Can you .... what your parents looked like when they were your age?
10 It's a complete .... who painted the picture on the wall.

3 Complete the text with the words from the box. There is one word you don't need.

create	hidden	imagination	imagine
magic	puzzle	solve	

Yesterday in class our teacher asked us to close our eyes. We had to [1]............................. that we were walking along the beach in the summer. She asked us to [2]............................. a picture of the beach in our minds. Then she told us to walk along the beach slowly, looking at everything very carefully. She said 'Somebody has [3]............................. something and you need to find it – it's part of a [4]............................. that you are trying to work out.' At first, nobody understood, but then I realised it was a bit like having to [5]............................. a maths problem. It was a really interesting way of using our [6]............................. !

EP Word profile *mind*

Match the questions and answers.

1	What's the matter with Jess?	....	**a**	Would you mind turning down the music? We can't sleep.
2	Yes, can I help you?	....	**b**	I haven't made up my mind yet.
3	Stacie did really well in her test, didn't she?	....	**c**	Mind you don't hit your head.
4	Which subjects are you going to do next year?	....	**d**	Sure! He won't mind at all!
5	Can I look for my book under the table?	....	**e**	Her mum changed her mind and won't let her come to the party.
6	Could I borrow Harry's book?	....	**f**	Yes, I know. She's got a brilliant mind.

READING

1 Write the name of each shape using the words in the box.

> rectangle   square   trapezium   triangle

1 ....   2 ....

3 ....   4 ....

2 Complete the text about the shapes in exercise 1 with the words in the box.

> distance   length   longer   opposite   sides

A triangle has three [1]............................ but the other shapes all have four. In a square, all the sides
are the same [2]............................ . In a rectangle, the two [3]............................ sides are the same length.
Two sides are always [4]............................ . In a trapezium, two of the sides are parallel, which means
the [5]............................ between them is the same all the way along, but the other two are not.

3 Read the text and choose the correct word for each space, as in the example.

A DIFFERENT KIND OF ROOM

Have you ever seen a film where [0]..A.. people are much bigger than others? To [1]....... this special
effect, the film [2]....... probably used an Ames room.

In an Ames room, two people can be [3]....... next to each other, but they [4]....... as if they are very
different sizes! The room [5]....... to be square but it isn't. It is actually a trapezium, [6]....... that the sides
are not the same length. Using an Ames room, things look bigger in some [7]....... of the room than in
others.

In the picture, [8]....... was taken at a museum in Edinburgh, you can see two people. The man [9].......
the left appears to be much smaller than the woman. However, the man is actually [10]....... away than
the woman.

0 A some	**B** every	**C** all	**D** each
1 A create	**B** happen	**C** imagine	**D** turn
2 A writer	**B** director	**C** star	**D** actor
3 A growing	**B** putting	**C** increasing	**D** standing
4 A watch	**B** notice	**C** look	**D** see
5 A exists	**B** shows	**C** seems	**D** becomes
6 A meaning	**B** understanding	**C** thinking	**D** asking
7 A pieces	**B** slices	**C** parts	**D** bits
8 A what	**B** which	**C** who	**D** when
9 A on	**B** in	**C** by	**D** at
10 A wider	**B** longer	**C** taller	**D** further

GRAMMAR Past simple passive

1 Write full sentences from these words using the past simple passive.

1 The first / Ames room / construct / Adlebert Ames Jr

....

2 It / build / 1946

....

3 An Ames room / create / for / the film star's / latest / film

....

4 The actor / tell / not / to move

....

5 This trick / use / many / films

....

6 My photo / take / Ames room / museum / San Francisco

....

2 Choose the correct verb form.

1 The race *was won* / *is won* by an Olympic runner.
2 Every night, the news on TV *is read* / *was read* by the same lady.
3 The firefighters *were called* / *are called* to the fire last night.
4 My Dad *was asked* / *is asked* to talk to the school about his job.
5 Every year, the poster for the music festival *are designed* / *is designed* by school.
6 Our school *was painted* / *is painted* by our parents every year.
7 That exercise *was done* / *is done* last week in class.
8 Fun things *was made* / *were made* in our weekly arts class.

3 Complete the second sentence so that it means the same as the first. Use between one and three words.

1 My grandfather built the house 50 years ago.
The house .... my grandfather 50 years ago.
2 Someone delivers our post every day.
Our post .... every day.
3 Our teacher didn't tell us about the new exams.
We .... about the new exams.
4 My friend did this painting.
This painting .... my friend.
5 Thieves stole my bag last Saturday.
My bag .... thieves last Saturday.
6 That place made interesting clothes.
Interesting clothes .... at that place.
7 Our team won the game.
The game .... our team.
8 They never cancelled flights from that airport.
Flights from that airport ....

4 Complete the text with the past simple passive form of the verbs in the box.

| base | call | direct | film | show | tell | write |

FILM REVIEW ✪ ✪ ✪ ✪

A film ¹............................ in our local cinema last week. It ²............................ *The Illusionist*. It ³............................ by Neil Burger. The story ⁴............................ on a short story called *Eisenhem the illusionist*. This story ⁵............................ by Steven Millhauser. My friend and I ⁶............................ the story by our teacher. According to one website, the story takes place in Austria but actually it ⁷............................ in the Czech Republic.

5 👁 Choose the correct sentence in each pair.

1 a We have been playing together since we were borned.
  b We have been playing together since we were born.
2 a It was my 15th birthday party, and the place where the party was organised was in a park.
  b It was my 15th birthday party, and the place where was organised the party was in a park.
3 a Many places in Jakarta were covered by water.
  b Many places in Jakarta was covered by water.
4 a He looked shy, but then I got to know him better, and was surprised of all the things we had in common.
  b He looked shy, but then I got to know him better, and was surprised by all the things we had in common.
5 a The first city that we visited was called Vielle.
  b The first city that we visited we call Vielle.

VOCABULARY   *make* and *let*

1 **Choose the correct verb.**

1 The magician *let / made* a young girl try a trick on her own.

2 Mum *let / made* me tidy my room before I went to the party.

3 The air steward *let / made* everyone listen to the security information.

4 I wanted to go to the party but my parents wouldn't *let / make* me.

5 Mum and Dad *let / made* us wait until midnight to open our presents.

6 Will you *let / make* me help you?

7 The band *let / made* the audience wait for an hour.

8 Our teacher *let / made* my friend help me with the exercise – usually she *lets / makes* us work on our own.

2 **Complete the conversation using the correct form of *let* or *make*.**

> **Bill:** How was your science test?

> **Tim:** It was OK, I think. But ¹............................ me do science at university!

> **Bill:** Your parents ²............................ you do anything you don't want to! They'll ³............................ you choose because they know it's your life!

> **Tim:** I know. Will they ⁴............................ me get a part-time job?

> **Bill:** I'm sure they will. Why don't you ask them? Why are you asking me all these questions?

> **Tim:** Oh, it's just that my friend's dad ⁵............................ him study law, and another friend's parents ⁶............................ him join a band, which is what he really wants to do – they ⁷............................ him study music at university.

> **Bill:** No one should ⁸............................ you do anything you don't want to. But I think most parents ⁹............................ their kids ¹⁰............................ their own choices. They just help them a bit!

LISTENING

1 **Match the words to their meanings.**

1 fold ....   **a** the paper is fixed along one side and can be used to cover

2 corner ....   **b** used to make candles and to protect things from water

3 flap ....   **c** the point which is formed by the meeting of two lines

4 wax ....   **d** bend a piece of the paper, so that one part of it lies flat on top of another part

2 ▶17 **Listen to a girl talking about a magic trick she does with a piece of a paper. What does she do?**

1 makes the paper disappear

2 makes something from the paper

3 makes a message appear on the paper

3 ▶18 **You will hear an interview with a boy, Jerry. For each question, choose the correct answer A, B or C.**

1 Who first encouraged Jerry to do magic tricks?
   A his aunt
   B a performer
   C his father

2 Jerry's ability to do magic tricks improved when he
   A had some private lessons.
   B watched a primary school teacher.
   C joined a special club.

3 What does Jerry do now to develop his ability?
   A He goes to live shows regularly.
   B He reads plenty of books on magic.
   C He finds videos of tricks online.

4 How do Jerry's parents feel about him leaving school early?
   A They are happy to give him money each month.
   B They would still like him to take all his exams.
   C They believe he will be successful in his career.

5 Jerry's most successful trick on the TV show was
   A changing pages into money.
   B making a card disappear.
   C hiding coins in his hands.

6 What does Jerry hope to do in five years' time?
   A open his own school
   B move to Russia for work
   C write a book on magic

Acknowledgements

Development of this publication has made use of the Cambridge English Corpus, a multi-billion word collection of spoken and written English. It includes the Cambridge Learner Corpus, a unique collection of candidate exam answers. Cambridge University Press has built up the Cambridge English Corpus to provide evidence about language use that helps to produce better language teaching materials.

This product is informed by English Profile, a Council of Europe-endorsed research programme that is providing detailed information about the language that learners of English know and use at each level of the Common European Framework of Reference (CEFR). For more information, please visit www.englishprofile.org

The authors and publishers acknowledge the following sources of copyright material and are grateful for the permissions granted. While every effort has been made, it has not always been possible to identify the sources of all the material used, or to trace all copyright holders. If any omissions are brought to our notice, we will be happy to include the appropriate acknowledgements on reprinting.

Photo Acknowledgements

p. 5: Pressmaster/Shutterstock; p. 11: Sonja Pacho/Corbis; p. 17: Sean Justice/Getty; p. 19: David De Lossy/Getty; p. 21: format4/Alamy; p. 22: Steve Bower/Shutterstock; p. 23: (B/L) Tory Kallman/Shutterstock, (B/R) rui vale souse/Shutterstock; p. 27: Cultura Creative/Alamy; p. 29: Lisa F. Young/Shutterstock; p. 31: prudkov/Shutterstock; p. 32: RapidEye/iStock; p. 33: bikeriderlondon/Shutterstock; p. 35: Bettmann/Corbis; p. 36: Jupiterimages/Getty; p. 37: Joos Mind/Getty; p. 41: MBI/Alamy; p. 43: Nitr/Shutterstock; p. 48: (T/L) Wang LiQiang/Shutterstock, (T/R) Elena Larina/Shutterstock, (B/L) Keith Szafranski/istock, (B/R) yoglimogli/getty; p. 49: Sheldon Levis/Alamy; p. 53: taryn/Getty; p. 57: CandyAppleRed/Macroimage/Alamy; p. 58: Snap Stills/Rex; p. 61: slobo/iStock; p. 67: (T) Alan Poulson Photography/Shutterstock, (B) Kerstin Waurick/iStock; p. 69: EXImages/Alamy; p. 73: Tetra Images/Alamy; p. 77: (T) Evan Birch/Getty, (T/ C) Blend Images/Alamy, (B/C) Iakov Filimonov/Shutterstock, (B) Apelöga/Getty; p. 81: Michael Doolittle/Alamy; p. 82: Snap Stills/Rex; p. 83: Tom Chance/Corbis.

Front cover photo by Leon van den Edisvag/Shutterstock.

Illustrations

Mark Duffin pp. 12 (B), 44, 59, 65, 76; Stuart Harrison pp. 8, 12 (T), 15, 16, 26, 28, 30, 47, 50, 55, 62, 66, 70; Alek Sotirovski (Beehive Illustration) pp. 4, 9, 20, 38, 51, 71, 75, 80.

The publishers are grateful to the following contributors:
text design and layouts: emc design Ltd; cover design: Andrew Ward; picture research: emc design Ltd; audio recordings: produced by IH Sound and recorded at DSound, London; edited by Helen Forrest.

Yesterday's Wir [barcode: C000056538]
No 9
from
Ellesmere Port to Bromborough
including
Whitby Great Sutton Little Sutton
Childer Thornton Hooton Eastham

A Cynicus postcard pposted in 1911

Design & Origination: Ian Boumphrey

Printed By: Bookprint Sl, Barcelona

Published By: Ian & Marilyn Boumphrey
The Nook 7 Acrefield Road Prenton Wirral CH42 8LD
Tel/Fax: 0151 608 7611   e-mail: ian@yesterdayswirral.co.uk
Web site: www.yesterdayswirral.co.uk

Front Cover: *Bromborough Cross*

ISBN 1-899241-13

**Price
£6.95**

CONTENTS

INTRODUCTION

For our ninth *Yesterdays Wirral* publication we are covering the south east part of the peninsula for the first time. Travelling from Ellesmere Port and Whitby through Great Sutton, Little Sutton, Childer Thornton, Hooton, Eastham, Bromborough and Bromborough Pool. Because we are covering a larger area than our previous publication, *Yesterday's Wirral No 8 – Bebington & the Mid Wirral Villages*, we have reverted to our normal A4 size book with 64 pages and have included over 135 illustrations. As with our previous *Yesterday's Wirral* publications, we have tried to feature pictures that have not been published before. In some of the smaller villages featured there is little written down information so we have relied more on information gleaned from talking to local residents, for which we are most grateful.

ACKNOWLEDGEMENTS

We would like to thank the following people for their contribution towards this publication: David Allan, The Bromborough Society, John Brown, Peter Helm, Gavin Hunter, Ron Jones, Jim Kenyon, D Morgan & Co, Brian Nicholson, Susan Nicholson, Albert Nute, and many other people who have helped us in any way with this publication.

All the photographs in this publication are from the author's collection with the exception of the 'D Morgan tipper at Bowaters' photograph (*page 20*) which was kindly loaned by Lorraine Dennan.

Ellesmere Port

Poole Hall, a perfect example of Tudor architecture, dated from at least 1574, this being the date stone above the fireplace in the Hall, and is thought could be some 30 years earlier. The octagonal turret, pictured to the left of the clock in the tower, was one of two either end of the east front of the Hall, which faced the River Mersey, one of which housed a Chapel. Once surrounded by a moat, the hall was built for Thomas Poole and was the seat of the Poole family who owned considerable properties in Wirral and were ardent catholics. A pit near the Hall was discovered in 1844 containing a quantity of swords and pistols which were probably concealed there during the Civil Wars. The land was sold to Bowaters for a paper mill in 1929 which came into production in 1931. The Hall was demolished 1937/38 to allow for Bowater's expansion, but some farm buildings remained until 1956, then they too were knocked down to make way for further Bowater mills. The clock in the centre of the gable, which was made in 1704, was restored and moved to Bowater's foyer.

Within the Rivacre Valley's 45 acres of public open space, the Rivacre Valley swimming pool was opened 1 August 1934 and is pictured here in the 1950s. Built at a cost of £12,000, it was an open-air, salt water pool designed in a letter 'T' with the 'head', pictured the far end, being separated from the 'leg' by an island rising a few inches above the water. Known as *the swimming pool in a garden*, it was open from May to September 10am to 9pm each day. The indoor pool, adjacent to Whitby Park in the town centre, was opened April 1969. Despite this the outdoor pool lasted until the 1980s. The Bowater's tower seen on the left was built near the site of *Poole Hall* (*see above*).

Bowaters Mersey Paper Mills Ltd, paper manufacturers, came to Netherpool, Ellesmere Port in 1929. This was an ideal site of 52 acres initially, increasing to 115 acres after the war, which was situated beside the Manchester Ship Canal, with access to the River Mersey and the Port of Liverpool. The previous industrial owners, British Dyestuffs, had installed a rail link with the dock waterfront which Bowaters utilised. The mills were built on the site and land of *Poole Hall* (*see page 3*). Production started in 1931 as a two-machine unit but, due to its initial success, a further two machines were brought into operation in 1933. Bowaters struck a deal with the local council; 100 out of a total of 232 of the new council houses being built on the Overpool Estate, being reserved for Bowaters employees and their families. During the Second World War, a newsprint machine was switched to kraft paper, a strong brown paper used for packing artillery shells. Following the success of this venture, a commercial use was made of this kraft paper when a sack mill was built here in 1951 and the remaining *Poole Hall* buildings were demolished. In 1956 a ground-wood mill to convert logs from British forests was constructed, helping to reduce the reliance on imported timber. Also in 1956, Bowaters joined with Scott Paper Company of the USA to form Bowater-Scott Corporation in Britain, manufacturing industrial and household disposable paper products. A factory was built for a new company, Bowater-Eburite Ltd, in 1958 to produce fibre-board cases from board made in the mills on site.

The floating dry dock, seen here in 1905, was known as the 'pontoon'. It had been built in Newcastle, towed to Ellesmere Port, and was operational from 18 October 1893. Vessels up to 5,000 tons could be repaired or maintained here. This was the first industry attracted to the area as a result of the building of the Manchester Ship Canal.

The vessel *Gevalia* is seen unloading its cargo of timber for WH Wilson and other timber merchants onto railway wagons at the Ellesmere Port docks. This private railway took the timber to sidings at Westminster Road.

Timber for WH Wilson is being unloaded from a 'flat' at the North Pier on the Manchester Ship Canal, Ellesmere Port. It was carried to their yard, on the corner of Westminster Road and Station Road, by horse and wagon (*see next page*). The mound seen in the background behind the 'flat's' flag was the site of Poole Hall Rocks where the spoil from the canal was deposited, creating an enormous man-made hill and is still known as Mount Manisty, named after the engineer whose idea it was.

This aerial view of Stanlow Oil Dock, opened in 1922, and Shell Oil Storage, was taken in the 1950s. This was an ideal site having deep water access to the River Mersey via the Manchester Ship Canal, situated on a solid sandstone outcrop and in an isolated position away from industrial and residential developments. It was also surrounded by undeveloped land owned by the Ship Canal company. The nearest of the two docks seen on the right was built in 1933.

The only places local children could swim before the Rivacre Swimming Pool was opened in 1934 (*see page three*) were on the shores of the River Mersey, in the 'cut' on the Shropshire Union Canal or, as seen here, on one of two small beaches on the Manchester Ship Canal which had not been altered by the cutting of the canal.

The two men standing by this Foden steam wagon in the early 1920s, which belonged to WH Wilson, Timber Merchant, Ellesmere Port, are Bill Vale and Harry Rose. The company was founded in 1887 and is thought to be the oldest local company still trading. Originally their premises were in Station Road, adjoining the Parish Church, and they then moved to this timber yard which was at the junction of Westminster Road and Station Road.

Above:
The horse-drawn timber wagon has arrived at Wilson's yard. The company moved from here to their present site on the Rossmore Industrial Estate in 1965, the same year that they added Ellesmere Port to the company title. John Nicholas Crescent today occupies part of the site.

Left:
Some of WH Wilson's employees are seen posing in fancy dress in front of the horse-drawn float.
The building behind was the former Police Station and Magistrates Court which was erected in 1911 at a cost of *c.*£6,000. The Police moved to their present Whitby Road premises in January 1970, with the Magistrates Court continuing operating here for some time.

Thomas Warrington & Sons, Builders & Contractors, were established in Ellesmere Port in 1892. Their office was at 82, Station Road and their works, seen here, were in King Street.
The local Borough Council reached an overspill agreement with the City of Liverpool in 1959 to assist with the housing and unemployment problems. They undertook to provide 5,500 dwellings in Ellesmere Port to house 20,000 people. Many of these homes were built by Thomas Warrington. They became a public company in 1964 and moved to the Rossmore Industrial Estate. They took over McAlpines in 1988, and were then operating from the Chester Business Park, which they owned, but ceased trading in 1991.

The *Railway Commercial Hotel*, Station Road, Ellesmere Port, is pictured *c.*1890 when John McGarva was the victualler. The hotel was built adjacent to the station (*see page 10*). A soldier in uniform can be seen among the group posing for the photographer.

The hotel seen above had changed its name to the *Station Hotel*, being pictured here in 1909, the year the extension on the right was added. A single storey extension was added onto the far side of the building in 1912 and the pub was later purchased by Birkenhead Brewery. The three men on the right have walked from the railway crossing whilst the horse-drawn water cart is heading for the station, the other side of the fence on the right (*see page 10*).

A wagon load of timber is heading for WH Wilson's yard, probably brought from North Pier on the Manchester Ship Canal (*see page 5*). The founder, Mr WH Wilson, died in 1935 with the business then being run by his two sons, Leslie and Edgar and more recently by Jim Kenyon. The company added Ellesmere Port to the company name in 1965. The two horses are passing in front of a branch of Parrs Bank in Westminster Road at the junction with Station Road, with the photographer standing at the entrance to Wilson's timber yard.

This view looking down Station Road was taken from Westminster Bridge, which was opened by Rt. Hon. Selwyn Lloyd, MP for Wirral, on 20 July 1961. The bridge replaced the railway crossing, and the cattle underpass was closed when the bridge was opened. The *Station Hotel* on the right is seen in both the photographs opposite and the building on the extreme left was Parrs Bank in Westminster road, seen in the picture above.

Ellesmere Port station is viewed from Westminster Bridge in the 1960s. The station, which opened 1 July 1863 on the Hooton to Helsby Railway, was originally known as Whitby Locks but changed its name to Ellesmere Port Station in 1870. The sidings to the right of the station buildings now from part of the station car park.

Looking along Whitby Road in the 1920s, this was the main shopping area. A garage is seen behind the two cars on the right. The row of buildings beyond the cars were the private houses seen on the next page, which have lost their front gardens and have been converted into shops. They were opened to fulfill the increased demand from the growing population of Ellesmere Port which had risen from 4,082 in 1901 to 13,063 by 1921 and to 18,911 by 1931.

This picture postcard, posted in 1911, depicts Whitby Road which was the main route through Ellesmere Port. Victoria Road is seen on the left and the cottages beyond, behind the trees, are all now shops (*see previous picture*). Opposite these cottages and set back is The *Knot Hotel* which can be seen in the photograph below.

The *Knot Hotel*, which can be seen in the Whitby Road photograph above, is pictured here *c.*1920. At this time the publican was John Winn who was still there in 1940. There used to be a bowling green at the back. In 1961 the Knot Hotel was a member of 'The Robley Group of Fine Hotels and Restaurants' and their advertising stated: *The Port's brightest and most friendly meeting place with 'live' entertainment every weekday evening in the music room, a luxurious lounge providing soft background music is available too. The* Knot *wine shop supplies wines and spirits of every description also Trumans Burton beers for your home needs.*

The iron building on the right in Enfield Road, known as the 'tin Church', was the Roman Catholic Church which opened 21 March 1909. A school was opened on a site to the right of the Church 4 November 1912 with 115 children on the register. As the parish grew so did the demand for a new Church and eventually the foundation stone was laid 28 September 1930. The new Church opened 12 October 1931 at the end of Enfield Road with the junction of Whitby Road (*see picture below*). The old Church was altered to provide schooling for 100 pupils. In 1983 the old Church and school were demolished and a new presbytery built on the site in 1984.

The foundation stone of Our Lady Star of the Sea was laid on 28 September 1930 and the Church, which is pictured on the left, was opened on the corner of Enfield Road and Whitby Road on 12 October 1931. Romanesque in style, it had accomodation for over 500 people and replaced the Church pictured above, which stood further down Enfield Road.

The Wesleyan Methodist Chapel and Sunday School were built here in Whitby Road in 1914 at a cost of £5,000. This 1928 photograph shows the backs of the houses on the left in Oldfield Road. Today the Church faces the main shopping area in Ellesmere Port.

The Ecclesiastical Parish of Ellesmere Port was formed 23 March 1871 from the Parish of Eastham. Christ Church, photographed here from Station Road with Worcester Street to the left, was erected in 1869 at a cost of £2,900 and had 330 sittings. Built of stone in the Early Decorated style the tower can be seen with a turret containing one bell. This Church replaced an earlier one of 1842.

This was an advertising postcard for the architects, contractors and furnishers of the *Grace Arms Hotel* in Stanney Lane. It was named after the Grace family who had an ancient seat at *Whitby Old Hall* which stood in Stanney Lane at the junction of Vale Road (*see caption below*).

There were two *Whitby Halls*, both in Staney Lane and were both owned by members of the Grace family. This is the more modern one *Whitby Hall*, built *c.*1860 and was purchased by the council in 1931. This housed the council offices with 41 acres of land laid out as a public park in 1933. The *Whitby Old Hall*, situated on the corner of Stanney Lane and Vale road, was a mansion of red brick with stone dressings in the Elizabethan style and was the ancient seat of the Grace family. During structural alterations in 1905 a store of more than 1,000 guineas of George II's reign was found in perfect condition in the beams. The building was demolished in the 1960s.

Whitby

Rose Cottage is pictured in Whitby Road at its junction with Arrowe Lane, which is to the left and now called Stanney Lane, in the early part of this century. This half timbered, thatched cottage was demolished to widen the road and the police station, which opened in January 1970 , stands on a site behind where this cottage is pictured.

Looking along Whitby Road towards Ellesmere Port, Whitby Post Office can be seen on the right at its junction with Vale Road. The Post Office, which was also a High Class Baker & Confectioners shop, was then run by WH Backhouse. The *Sportsman's Arms* pictured on the left dates back to at least 1831 when the victualler was Mr Hough who was also a coal merchant and the pub was then known as the *Dog & Partridge*. Pictured here in 1924, the side of the pub advertises a Bowling Green & Billiards, when the publican was Joseph Bond (it is still known as 'Bondy's by some locals) and the owners were West Cheshire Brewery of Tranmere. They were taken over by Threlfalls in 1927 who in turn were acquired by Whitbreads Brewery in 1967. The pub today bears no resemblance to the one in this photograph.

Post Office corner, which is also in the previous picture, can be seen in the background in this 1950s photograph. The Post Office had moved and the old building was then occupied by Mellor's Bakery. Due to the increase in population there was a demand for new shops and the seemingly new premises on the right are only the old buildings with new fronts. Pooltown Road is off to the left.

The caption on the postcard above, which was published by 'Wallis' of Ellesmere Port and posted in 1914, states 'Garden City'. This is a view of Pooltown Road, Whitby and shows open fields to the left with undeveloped land opposite the front of the houses. The name 'Garden City' was apparently given to these properties, which are still there today and number from 115, as they were so unlike any other in the area. The picture below is also Pooltown Road but taken in 1931 when the houses on the right were newly built and there is no pavement whereas further down the road the pavement starts by the old houses.

Ellesmere Port & District Cottage Hospital is seen here in Whitby Road *c.*1930. The building was originally known as *Heathfield House* and was owned by the Mansfield family who had a gas distribution business in Oxford Street, Ellesmere Port and a works in Birkenhead, being famous for the their invention of Calor Gas. The property was first used as a hospital – for the military, during World War One, closing down at the end of hostilities. In 1919 this building and 12 acres of land were donated by the Cheshire Public House Trust and converted into a hospital. The building then had two windows either side and one above the front entrance porch. The extensions, eight windows on the left and the flat roof to the right, which included a maternity unit, were carried out in the 1920s. Today it is known as the Ellesmere Port Hospital, Wirral & West Cheshire Community NHS Trust and the garden pictured here is now the car park.

Ellesmere Port County Grammar School for Boys, which opened September 1959, is pictured here in Chester Road, Whitby, with the Girls Grammar School being opened in Sycamore Drive in 1961. Prior to the grammar schools opening, all pupils in the Ellesmere Port area who were successful in their 11+ exams, thus qualifying for a grammar school place, had to travel to Helsby, Chester, Bebington or West Kirby.

Great Sutton

The Church of St John the Evangelist, which was consecrated 24 November 1879 for a new Parish and had seating for 240 persons, is seen from Chester Road with Church Lane off to the right between the Church and the railings. The first Vicar was Rev Charles Mayall from 1879 to 1900 then Rev Percy Douglas. Initially the Church and school shared the same building when Mrs Dunbabin was the schoolmistress. This was the main road through Great Sutton, before the new road was built, with *New Hey* (*pictured on page 20*), behind the photographer.

The *White Swan Inn,* which can also be seen in the picture opposite, dates back to at least 1850 when the victualler was Edward Horne who was also a farmer. This was a fully licenced pub and the *Bull's Head* (seen in the next two pictures) was only a beerhouse. The *White Swan* is still there today and is now owned by Burtonwood Brewery. *Mount Farm*, the white building on the left behind the telegraph pole, was demolished (the last farmer being Bill Mason) and a health centre built on the site.

Looking down Chester Road, Great Sutton towards Chester in the early part of this century, when this was the main road from Birkenhead to Chester. The sign for the *Bulls Head Inn* can be seen half way down on the left beyond the barn and the parish Church spire is in the distance (*see page opposite*).

This photograph was taken looking in the other direction along Chester Road, Great Sutton towards Birkenhead. In the distance to the right of the white building is the White Swan (*see opposite page*). The ladies posing by the wall on the right are in front of the *Bulls Head,* which can also be seen on the left in the picture above. This beerhouse, which was not fully licensed, dates back to at least 1850 when Matthew Bough was the beerhouse keeper. Up to the last days of this old pub, the landlord would spread sawdust onto the floor and spitoons would be provided. It was replaced with a new pub in 1926, which was sited behind the wall on the right, and the old *Bulls Head* building became a private residence. The brewery decided *c.*1965 that a new pub was needed and the '1926' *Bull's Head* together with the original pub building, pictured here, with four cottages behind it, were demolished, to accommodate the car park for the third *Bulls Head* built to replace the second one.

New Hey is pictured on the bend in Chester Road, Great Sutton, just around the corner from the Church, seen on the previous page. The gate on the right led to a field where Captain and Mrs Stevenson kept polo ponies. D Morgan Plant Hire Ltd, which was founded in 1950 by Denis and Ursula Morgan, moved to *New Hey* in 1965 where its head office is located today. Their first contract was hauling sand for the new runways at Hooton Aerodrome (*see page 34*) where Denis loaded his lorry by hand, delivering two loads each day. The early 1950s saw the further development of Bowaters paper mill (*see page 3*) which was to be the springboard for the company's growth (*see below*).

The dragline excavator is loading a D Morgan tipper truck at Bowaters in 1958. This was where the company's business took off in the 1950's (*see above*). In 1974 the proprietor's son, also called Denis, joined the family business. Following a long illness, Denis senior died in 1978. During the early 1980s major acquisitions were made including old quarries for landfill sites. They continued to diversify settting up Brock, a building and civil engineering company, and Wirral Waste, a waste disposal skip hire company. Today the company owns and operates one of the largest earthmoving and tipper fleets in the country. Recent contracts have included Manchester Airport and Vauxhalls.

Little Sutton

In 1896 James Henry Coulter is described as a Boot & Shoe Manufacturer at *Liverpool House* Chester Road, Little Sutton. His wife is seen standing outside their single storey *shop c.1906*. The shop was later purchased by JD Basnett, also a boot & shoe manufacturer but by the 1930s these premises had become a newsagent & confectioner's, although still owned by the Basnett family (*see photograph below*). Some schoolchildren, on the left, pose for the photographer.

The shoe shop, which is pictured above, is seen on the right in the 1950s and has now become Basnett's newsagents & confectioners shop, with the poles still supporting the original canopy. The shops beyond the house with the garden are Betty's and Irwins grocery store. Today the newsagents shop has been demolished and also several buildings beyond.

The *Black Lion Inn* can be seen at the entrance to Little Sutton in Chester Road looking towards Birkenhead. Pictured here in the 1890s, when the victualler was Richard Purcell who was also a butcher, the inn dates back to 1754 when it was a fully licensed coach house. It was once one of the coaching inns between Chester and Birkenhead which lost most of its trade when the Birkenhead to Chester Railway opened in 1840. In 1933 plans were approved to rebuild the pub further back from the road, in order to eliminate the 'bottleneck'. However, for some reason, this was never carried out. In 1969, despite members of the Ellesmere Port Council fighting to preserve this old building, the then brewers, Walker Cain Ltd, replaced it with a larger modern pub set back from the road. This formed part of the redevelopment of Little Sutton with new shops and parking facilities. To the rear of the building were the old stables, the original coach house (which was used as a beer cellar) and a centuries old horse trough.

This photograph, taken prior to 1910, shows Lockett's Bakery and Corn Factors shop on the corner of Ledsham Road. Due to the increase in population the building beyond Locketts was converted into three shops and a new building, which is currently a 'charity' shop, was erected between that and the next building which was a Presbyterian Church, built in 1851. All the buildings beyond the Church on the right have since been demolished, with most of the buildings on both sides of the road having lost their gardens and the road has been widened (*see pictures on previous and next page*).

Looking along Chester Road, the building on the corner of Ledsham Road seen in the previous picture, is behind the car on the right. The gardens in front of the properties in the distance on both sides of the road have been taken away and the road widened. The shops to the right of the nearest car, which are set back, have a 1932 date stone. To the left of the light coloured car is now Walkers Lane, named after the chemist and local photographer whose shop can be seen in the picture below.

Taken from Ledsham Lane, the shop on the right is in Chester Road, the main highway through Little Sutton, with Walkers Lane down the side of the shop. The lane is named after a Mr Walker who traded as a chemist from that shop and also sold picture postcards he had taken of the local area [some of which we have used in this book, including two on page 41 which show his wife in their pony & trap]. The car on the other side of the road is standing outside Laura Knowles, Drapery shop and the van on this side of the main thoroughfare belonged to TH Lowes, Butcher.

Sutton was an intermediate station on the Hooton to Helsby line which opened 1 July 1863. As there was already a station called Sutton on the Birkenhead to Chester railway, that station then changed its name to Ledsham and this one became Sutton. In 1886 it changed its name to Little Sutton. This 1914 photograph shows the train leaving towards Ellesmere Port and waiting to the left of the red sandstone station buildings is a chauffeur-driven car. The shop in the background is now No 41 Station Road.

This was one of two postcards taken by Little Sutton photographer, P Walker (see previous page), of local volunteers, mainly for the Cheshire Regiment, who are posing on Little Sutton station platform prior to enlisting for the military in September 1914. By Christmas of that year most of them were fighting in France; many of them never returned. Note the Birkenhead Brewery advertisement in the background between the windows. Today the station is no longer manned and the station buildings, which are now closed, are in need of restoration.

Looking from Chester Road down Station Road, Little Sutton Railway Station can be seen in the distance. Sutton Motor Company, who advertise as 'Automobile Engineers' and who are 'Commercial Vehicle Experts', are seen on the right. Today the garage trades as 'Hollywood Car Sales' which was established in 1961. The Police Station, which is on the left with a flagpole in front, closed in 1947 and Little Sutton was then covered from Ellesmere Port. The building is used as offices today. The vehicle on the left is delivering to the *Old Red Lion (see next page)*. The first building beyond the Police Station in Station Road, behind the flagpole, was the Little Sutton Reading Room. This single storey building is used today as the headquarters for the Ellesmere Port & District Red Cross.

The *Railway Inn,* once a Birkenhead Brewery pub, is pictured here in the 1890's taken from Chester Road, Little Sutton, when the licensee was Thomas Worthington who was 'Licensed to Sell by Retail, Ale & Porter'. The last pint was served here on 21 March 1972 when the then owners, Whitbread Brewery, decided to call 'time'. The houses in Heath Court on the corner of Heath Lane and Chester Road, were later built on the site *(see next page)*.

The Wirral Harriers were originally the province of Sir Thomas Stanley's foxhounds. However, when that was given up, the chase continued but in a rather desultory way until a new pack was formed in 1868. They are seen meeting in front of the *Old Red Lion* (*see below & opposite*) at the turn of the century. The pub dates back to at least 1850 when Mary Tyrell was the victualler. Not only did the Eastham Benefit Friendly Society hold its meetings here but they also owned the property for which they received £50 annual rent. The Little Sutton Loyal Victoria Lodge of Oddfellows was formed in 1888, taking over the assets of the friendly society. The Oddfellows borrowed money, using the *Old Red Lion* as collateral, to build eight cottages in Red Lion Lane. This meant that they then had a weekly income and in 1899 the West Cheshire Brewery bought the pub at auction for £5,500. Rock Ferry Cycle Co works is seen on the left which later had an extension built towards Heath Lane. The new building is pictured below, beyond the brewery wagon.

This panoramic view is looking down Chester Road, Little Sutton, in the direction of Childer Thornton and shows the 'old' *Old Red Lion* in the centre of the picture and the 'new' *Ye Olde Red Lion* to the right. This photograph was officially taken for the Birkenhead Brewery in 1934, about the time when the new pub replaced the old one (*see*

The crowd has gathered to see the Prime Minister, Mr Asquith, who was visiting Little Sutton on 20 July 1912. The people are well behaved, especially as there are no barriers and not a policeman in sight. The single-storied building in the background was an extension to the *Old Red Lion*, which was known locally as the 'Oddfellows Hall' – as this is where the Oddfellows met (*see details in caption opposite*) – or the 'cow shed'. According to locals, dances were held here every Saturday night. This part of the pub was demolished first to make way for the building of the new *Ye Olde Red Lion* whilst the *Old Red Lion* kept trading. In order to comply with the then licensing laws the licence had to pass overnight from the old to the new pub the following morning. If this did not happen the licence would be lost. The picture below was probably taken just before the licence had passed to the new premises as the pub sign is still above the old premises. After the *Old Red Lion* was demolished the road, which was then widened, passed through the site of the old pub.

picture above). The altered *Railway Inn* can be seen on the extreme left and the Police Station is on the right with the Little Sutton Reading Rooms beyond (*see page 25*). The Police Station closed in August 1947 when responsibility for Little Sutton passed to the police based at Ellesmere Port. The building was later used for offices.

Childer Thornton

Thornton Hall, pictured in Chester Road, Childer Thornton, dates back to at least 1850 when Wm. Stockley Esq was the owner. The hall estate, which included 13 acres of land, outbuildings, lodge and four cottages, was put up for auction by John Briscoe in 1885 although according to Sulley's *The Hundred of Wirral* (1889*)* JJ Briscoe was still there, but by 1895 it was in the name of Wm. Shone. In the 1920s/30s the owner was Major A Harold Bibby DSO, Chairman of Bibby Line1935-69 and later knighted. More recently it has become an hotel changing ownership and names quite frequently - in 1987 it was called the *St Andrews' Hotel* which had previously been the *Regency Hotel* and within six months had become a *Bernie Inn!* At that time it was described as having 47 ensuite bedrooms. Today it is called *Burleydam*.

The *White Lion* is pictured in Heath lane in the 1890s when Fred Elcock was the publican and it was then owned by Birkenhead Brewery. It dates back to at least 1859 when Joseph Ashton was the beerhouse keeper. The pub, which is still there today, is somewhat bigger but still maintains its character.

Residents of Childer Thornton are posing for the cameraman in Chester Road on Coronation Day 22 June 1911. Next to the gentleman on the right, who is brandishing a sword, is the band with their instruments and then the local children who are wearing fancy dress. The buildings from the right were: Swift's butchers shop; Hodgsons - provisions, (who also had a shop in Bromborough). Both these shops were demolished c1960s; *The Original Half-Way House* which was owned by Yates Brewery (founded in Manchester in 1886, sold to John Smiths in 1961 and currently owned by Burtonwood Brewery). In 1859 the victualler was Mary Pearson and it was a fully licensed pub. In 1828 the pub was called the *Hare & Hounds*; The *Rifleman's Arms* next door, dating back to at least 1889, was owned by Chester Northgate Brewery (founded in 1870 and taken over by Greenhall Whitley, Warrington, in 1949), but only had a beer licence. It was closed in 1969 and the building demolished c.1982. Beyond that were Childer Thornton Post Office then School Lane and Lockley's Sweet & Confectionery shop (*also see picture below*).

These are the same buildings seen in the photograph above but taken from the other direction. The gentleman on the left is walking down New Road in front of the cobblers, having just passed Ye Olde Village Store which was also the Post Office. The *Rifleman's Arms* has a sign above the door and the large building beyond, the *Halfway House* (Halfway between Chester and Birkenhead), is said to be one of the most haunted buildings on the Wirral Peninsula.

Hooton Parish Church, seen in the background, was erected in 1858 for Mr RC Naylor, a wealthy Liverpool banker and the owner of *Hooton Hall*, as a tribute to his wife. Designed by J Colling, the architect for the extension to *Hooton Hall*, it was built in Norman / Italian style at a cost of £5,000 and is described as one of the most spectacular Churches in Wirral. The lodge and entrance gate to *Hooton Hall* with unfluted ionic columns between them are repeated on the right to form a semi-circle. The war memorial was erected 'To the Honoured Memory of the Men From Hooton, Childer Thornton and Little Sutton'. There is a list of 35 who died in World War One and later the 43 men who fell in World War Two were added.

The eventual winner of the New Ferry Tradesmen's Walk is seen passing along Chester Road through Hooton closely followed by the 'bowler hatted' judges on bicycles. The men in the background are standing outside Marston's Cycle Works which by 1923 had become S Bartley & Co, Motor Cycle Agents. By 1934 it was occupied by John F Williams who was a motor engineer. The building, which was at the junction of Chester Road and Welsh Road, was demolished and a petrol station and garage built on the small site. However, the garage was closed for many years but has recently reopened.

Hooton

Hooton Hotel in Neston Road dates back at least to 1859 when it was listed as the *Hooton Arms* with William Bake as the victualler. It was probably built in the 1840s after Hooton station opened in September 1840. The top photo was taken in the 1890s when Arthur Bagnall was the publican and a sign advertises the newsroom on the right which is where the locals would gather to obtain the latest news. Business must have been good as by the early 1900s, an extension had been built as can be seen in the middle photo and the whole building redesigned. The hotel sign is now seen between the chimneys which could be viewed from the station platform and passing trains. The lower 1950s view shows the hotel has recently been decorated and Threlfalls sign is on a middle gable. There was a bowling green to the right of the hotel, now part of the car park, and pigeon fanciers met in the loft of the old stables. Today it is a Beefeater restaurant and pub.

Hooton was an intermediate station on the Birkenhead to Chester railway which opened 23 September 1840. on 1 July 1863 a line opened from Hooton to Helsby with intermediate stations at Sutton (became Little Sutton 1886) and Whitby Locks (renamed Ellesmere Port 1870). The line still operates today. The Hooton to Parkgate line, opened 1866, was extended to West Kirby 1886 and closed 1962. The site of the line to West Kirby became the Wirral Way, Britain's first Country Park, opening in 1973. Hooton Brickworks' chimney is in the background.

This is the picture side of a postcard sent by Cyril Woods of No 5 Platoon 2nd Company - 2nd City Battalion Kings Regiment stationed at Hooton Park, to his cousin – on 10 October 1914. In his message he says:
This is a group of us before going off on a Sunday. We are having a fine time. We have to get up at six and go for a run round the racecourse. Lights out at 10.15. We have been doing rifle drill this last week. Yesterday we went for a two and a half hours route march with the band . . .
He goes on to describe their quarters (*see page 34*) and the views over the ship canal.

The *Hooton Hall* pictured here was built in 1788 replacing the original imposing half-timbered building which was erected in 1488 for the Egerton family. It stood in Hooton Park which covered some 1,000 acres. This Hall was designed by James Wyatt in the Adam style and built of Storeton stone with Italian style additions being made in the 19th century. One of its most 'colourful' owners was Sir William Stanley, Bart., who was a keen sportsman and friend of Louis Napoleon who became Napoleon III. The Hooton Estate was bought at auction in the late 1840s by a banker, Christopher Naylor and during this, its most glamourous period the hall contained 32 bedrooms, many servants and a beerhouse. In 1875 its contents were sold at auction and the hall later became derelict and untenanted for some years. At the end of the century a social and racing club came from Parkgate and was called the Hooton Park Club. Horse races, polo matches and croquet tournaments were held here. The last race was Boxing Day 1916, by which time the military had taken over the Hall and estate.

On 15 September 1914 Hooton Park including the Hall was offered to the military by the Hooton Park Club for training purposes with the Liverpool Pals being posted here. Two officers are seen with a group of new recruits who are still dressed in 'civies'. Behind the far group of Pals, who have been issued with rifles, can be seen the stone bridge over Rivacre Road which connected the stables with the Hall and racecourse. There were two bridges over Rivacre Road. This one was demolished mid 1950s and the other, which was situated nearer Ellesmere Port, a few years later. The clock tower on the right was only demolished a few years ago, due to its poor condition.

This view of Hooton Hall stables, with the clock tower in the background (*see page 33*), was taken in September 1914. In Cyril Woods' postcard sent in October 1914 (*see page 32*) he comments that their quarters were in the stables and were very comfortable [presumably the horses were not there!] The mens' kit can be seen on the left and rifles on the right. The brick wall behind the stables is still standing today.

Hooton Aerodrome, set in the grounds of Hooton Park, can be seen from the air *c.*1930. It was Cheshire's first airfield, opening as a training depot for fighter pilots with the Royal Flying Corps in 1917 and later Americans were stationed here (it was they who caused a fire which almost destroyed the Hall). Many of the frail planes crashed in the local countryside and graves of the airmen, some American, can be seen in Eastham churchyard. The airfield closed in 1919 reopening for flying in 1927 and by 1930 was the official airport for Liverpool until Speke Aerodrome was opened July 1933. In 1929 Edward, Prince of Wales, landed here on route to the Arrowe Park Scout Jamboree. An air service from Hooton to Dublin and Cork commenced August 1933. Two aircraft manufacturers, Comper Aircraft Co Ltd and Pobjoy Airmotors Ltd operated from here between 1929 and 1934. In 1936 a light bomber squadron in the Auxiliary Air Force was formed here. The RAF took over the aerodrome in October 1939 with Avro Ansons posted here for convoy duty over the Irish sea. Aircraft parts shipped over from USA were assembled here and at the end of the war hundreds of surplus aircraft were scrapped. The Cheshire Show was held here from 1959 –72. Vauxhalls obtained planning permission for a car factory on part of the site in 1960 with the first car being assembled here in 1962. The River Mersey is seen top right; Aircraft hangers in the centre; below them is the circular drive leading to the site of the Hall and above the remains of the Hall, can be seen the outline of the racecourse.

Eastham

Eastham windmill was originally sited in Carlett Park but in 1834 it was taken down and moved to this Chester side of Eastham Village. One of the sails was blown off during a gale in the last century so the miller removed the opposite sail. This worked well until a storm in 1895 blew the remaining two down and the miller used them to repair his other mill at Willaston. This is how the mill looked without any sails at the turn of the century. The mill was demolished in the 1930s. In 1932 a transport cafe was built on a site adjoining the mill by Cartwright Bros. of Little Sutton for George Sanderson and in the early 1970s it became a Little Chef with a motel being added later.

Above: Lady Vernon is about to place the mothers' and widows' wreath at the foot of Eastham War Memorial. There are 35 names of those who gave their lives in World War One and 31 in World War Two.

Left: The exact age of the old Eastham yew tree, which is sited in the churchyard of Eastham Parish church, is unknown. However, it is traced back at least 1,400 years to Saxon times when yew trees were encouraged to be grown in churchyards as the men used the branches of this tree to make their bows.

Below: Another view of Eastham War Memorial.

The band are resting outside the school in Stanley Lane (*see below*), in this Coronation Day procession 22 June 1911. St Mary's Parish Church of Eastham, which dates from the late 12th or early 13th centuries, can be seen on the left. The fine broach spire was completed in 1320 and restored in 1752 without alteration. The Church has been extended and restored over the centuries with much work done in Victorian times.

The girls and boys of Eastham are posing for the photographer *c.*1918 in front of their school buildings which date back to 1852. Erected at a cost of £1,000, which included a residence for the headmaster, they replaced the original school. This was situated in a converted barn attached to what became the *Hooton Arms* and was then the headmaster's residence. Due to rising numbers, the school was enlarged several times over the years and is now St Mary's C of E Primary School.

Looking down Stanley Lane, the *Stanley Arms* on the right, which was originally a farmhouse converted into an inn *c.*1840, was completely rebuilt and enlarged in 1891/92. This included the Stanley Crest which was carved in stone and can still be seen above the door today, a reminder of the family connection with *Hooton Hall*. The bunting, gentlemen on horses and carriages are all a sign of Miss Babington's and Rev H Barker's Wedding Day 24 June 1913 (*see next page*). Miss Babington was a keen horsewoman and rode with the Cheshire Hunt. The ladies in the distance are standing in the doorways of the buildings pictured below. The white wall on the right is the corner of a cottage which adjoined *Laurel Cottage* (*see photo opposite*) and was demolished in the 1950s.

The last cottage on the right in Stanley Lane with a datestone of 1699, which has numerous ladies and children outside, is also pictured above on the same day – Miss Babington's and Rev H Barker's Wedding Day. To the left of the white building on the other end of this row of cottages is a building facing down the road which used to be the Post Office and the left cottage of the white building behind the car is now *The Hay Loft*.

The original village inn stood opposite the *Hooton Arms*, pictured here *c.*1906 at the junction of Eastham Village Road and Ferry Road. It was later moved to an old farm at the side of *Eastham House* (dated 1691) which is now an old people's home. Before becoming an inn, the *Hooton Arms* was the schoolmaster's house with the school being sited in an adjoining, ancient barn with thatched roof and mud floor. In 1852 a new village school and adjoining master's house was built on land donated by Mr Naylor (*see page 37*), the owner of *Hooton Hall*, and by 1860 the former master's house had become the *Hooton Arms* beerhouse, when Catherine Hazlehurst was the victualler. The pub would have benefited from the extra trade brought from men employed on the construction of the Manchester Ship canal from 1887 to 1894. Birkenhead Brewery bought the *Hooton Arms* some years later and today it is owned by Whitbread Brewery. Note the 'rubbing stones' on the corner of the building to protect it from the wheels of vehicles.

The bride, Miss Babington, and groom, Rev Barker, are pictured on their wedding day 24 June 1913. The wedding was a sensation at the time as Miss Babington was a 'confirmed spinster' and the Rev Barker a widower, his first wife having died tragically when her skirt had caught fire as she was cooking and burnt to death. The newly weds are pictured in front of the 'shanty boys'.
They were named after the 'shanty' which was a building in a field behind Miss Harriet Shone's house in *Cropper's Nook*, Village Road, close to the entrance to the old recreation ground. The young men played billiards; whist drives were held here and in the summer cricket & tennis teas were served after matches. In 1945 the wooden building with corrugated iron roof was destroyed by fire (a former choir boy remembers stopping on his way to Church to see the fire extinguished).

This view was taken in Stanley Lane at the turn of the century. The Eastham Village School is seen behind the four boys on the right with a flagpole in front (*see page 38*). The other boys are sitting on a sandstone outcrop in front of *Laurel Cottage*. St Mary's Parish Church is behind the wall on the right (*see page 37*).

The bridesmaids are pictured at the wedding of Miss Sybil Torr to Frank Newall Watson on 1 August 1907. Sybil was Rev Torr's second daughter of four. Rev William Edward Torr inherited *Carlett Park* when his father, John, died in 1880, the same year he was appointed Vicar of Eastham and was licensed to live at the family home by the Bishop of Chester. In 1911 he was made a Canon of Chester Cathedral. Much loved by the villagers, especially the children, he organised a 'treat' each June when the band led the children from the village to a field near his home at *Carlett Park* where he arranged races, games and food. He died in 1924.

The side entrance to *Carlett Park* is to the left of *The lodge* in Ferry Road. *The Lodge* was badly damaged by bombs in 1941 and demolished (luckily the occupants were in their air raid shelter and were unhurt). The estate was purchased in 1846 by William Laird from Sir Thomas Stanley who was obliged to sell off the land to pay for his extragavent life style. John Torr, MP for Liverpool, bought the estate and built the mansion in 1859/60 and it then passed to his eldest son William (*see previous picture*). The estate was purchased by the Catholic Community of the Christian Brothers in Liverpool. It was occupied by the military during World War Two and sold to Cheshire County Education Committee in 1948 for £10,000.

Above:
Looking down Ferry Road, Eastham *c.*1905 with Lock Road on the right where the shed advertises a 'covered bicycle stand'. The pony and trap on the left probably belongs to the photographer F Walker of Little Sutton, whose wife is sitting in the trap, which is also seen in the photograph above taken by him. Further down the road towards the ferry is WG Pearson's sign for 'Private Field For Sports' and he also owned the tea rooms whose white house with tall chimneys is also seen in the picture on the left.

Left:
The tea rooms, pictured above in Ferry Road, are here called *Greenwood* (after the setting) and together with the adjoining stalls are ready for the 'invasion' of visitors, as seen in this postcard which was posted in 1922.

Eastham Ferry Hotel, pictured on the right, was built by Sir Thomas Stanley in 1846 replacing a much less splendid building. The first victualler then was Henry Nicholls. The hotel was built to encourage visitors to Eastham after the opening of the Birkenhead to Chester Railway had routed all the Chester to Liverpool trade via the ferry from Birkenhead. The hotel has survived and although it was a listed building, in 1978 the then owners, Burtonwood, demolished the splendid verandah. The two interior photographs below of the *Eastham Ferry Hotel* were taken from a 1950s postcard.

WEDNESDAY, MAY 4th, 1927.

9-30 p.m. to 2-30 a.m.

WIRRAL
POLO
CLUB

SIXTH

ANNUAL DANCE

EASTHAM FERRY BALLROOM.

This was a Ladies Dance Card for the Wirral Polo Club Annual Dance 4 May 1927 held at the Eastham Ferry Ballroom in the hotel grounds. The club was formed in 1876 using a field behind the *Eastham Ferry Hotel*, moving first to Clatterbridge then in 1900 to Hooton Park. The club disbanded in 1933.

Another view of the Jubilee Arch on the right, which was a copy of Marble Arch in London and acted as the entrance to Eastham Ferry gardens. It was originally erected in London Road for Queen Victoria's visit to Liverpool for her Jubilee in 1897. To the left of the arch is the *Eastham Ferry Hotel* and then the ballroom, which was burnt down in 1958. The cost for entrance to the attraction, was 2d (1p) in 1908, when 111,202 people patronised the gardens. The entertainments inside included Fred Brook's Vaudeville & Circus Co., (pictured below), a bear pit, ballroom, zoological gardens, menagerie, pierrot theatre, sideshows and tea rooms. Blondin, the famous tight-rope walker, visited Eastham several times performing his daring feats.

Fred Brook's Vaudeville & Circus Co. is entertaining the audience in the Eastham Ferry Hotel Gardens in 1908.

This Looping-the-loop ride at Eastham was estimated at reaching speeds of 95mph but the public were said to be genuinely too scared and too frightened to ride in the cars. It ended up as a gaunt, rusty skeleton.

This view from the top of the Jubilee Arch (*see previous two pages*) was taken *c.*1926. It shows how popular Eastham still was then with the paddle steamer *Saphire* arriving with a full boatload of visitors. The *Eastham Ferry Pier Bar*, pictured on the left, was originally called the *Tap Room* and was only a beerhouse. It is still pulling pints today and is called the *Ferry Inn*. The building behind the flag pole on the right dates back to 1857 and is pictured below.

This was probably an ARP exercise at Eastham Ferry during the Second World War with the men wearing fully protective clothing and gas masks. The building in the background has a date stone of 1857 and is the only ferry building still standing. It is still used for toilets today as it was in the picture above, seen behind the flagpole in 1926.

The site of 'Job's Ferry', the first landing point at Eastham, was some 300 yards north of *Eastham Ferry Hotel* and was established by the Chester monks in 1509. This was the main route for goods and people between the South, Wales, Chester and Liverpool. In 1790 two sailing boats left Liverpool every day, two hours before high water, for Eastham carrying goods and also a stage coach en route to Chester. In 1816 an engine driven packet boat the *Princess Charlotte* was put into service and instead of taking up to half a day, the journey now took about two hours and three years later the *The Old Lady,* another power propelled packet came into service followed by the *Maria* (named after Lady stanley and her daughter Maria). There were four trips a day then with prices much reduced and Eastham experienced a boom period. However, in 1840 the Chester to Birkenhead Railway was opened and caused a drastic reduction in Eastham's traffic. Due to Eastham's natural beauty, the boats still ran bringing visitors rather than goods and people passing through. One of the first improvements was the *Eastham Ferry Hotel* built by Sir Thomas Stanley in 1846 (*see page 42)*, replacing an old inn. Then in 1874 the lessees of the *Eastham Ferry Hotel*, Messrs Thompson & Gough, built this iron pier opposite their hotel and developed the gardens, which helped to bring more visitors to Eastham. Three paddle steamers offering a service to Liverpool came into operation at the end of the century (*see picture below)*.

The paddle boat, *Ruby,* pictured here, together with her sister boats, the *Pearl & Saphire,* were brought into service at the end of the century, replacing the older boats. Built by J Jones & Co of Garston, Liverpool, they helped to bring more visitors to Eastham. During the first World War they were taken over by the admiralty and converted for mine-sweeping duties. They resumed the service in 1919 but their condition had deteriorated and the service was withdrawn in 1930 with the pier being demolished in 1934/35 as it was considered a dangerous obstacle in the River Mersey.

This is an aerial view of Eastham Locks, the entrance to the Manchester Ship, taken in the 1940s. The reason for building the Manchester Ship Canal was to give access from the River Mersey for sea-going ships to the Port of Manchester. Work started on the project in November 1887 and the Eastham to Ellesmere Port section of the canal was flooded 19 June 1891 with the entire length of 35 miles being opened officially by Queen Victoria on 21 May 1894. Here at Eastham the channel of the Mersey was dredged to a depth of 30 feet at high water neap tides and 40 feet spring tides. The three locks pictured are divided by 30 feet concrete piers on which the hydraulic machinery to work the locks is located. The locks vary from 600 feet long by 80 feet wide on the land side; 350 feet by 50 feet in the middle and 150 feet by 30 feet on the river side. There are storm gates for each lock to be closed in rough weather. When opened ocean going ships up to 6,000 tons could pass through the canal. The capital raised for this undertaking was over £15 million.

This photograph was taken from the banks of the Manchester Ship Canal at Eastham showing the first and largest of the three locks which are also seen in the aerial photograph above.

Plymyard Tower was situated on the East side of Plymyard Avenue. In 1934 a directory shows that it had been converted into six flats. The ARP made use of its tall tower bringing it into service as a base and look-out during the Second World War. Said to be the first building locally to have central heating, it was demolished in 1976.

Plymyard Cottages, of which there were five, stood near *Plymyard Manor* and were the homes of labourers on the Plymyard Estate. When Kilburn Avenue was built in the 1930s, the new houses were built around them leaving them between Nos 16 & 18. The cottages, which faced the road, had long narrow gardens but due to the potential value of the land for these 'two up, two down' picturesque dwellings, they were demolished *c.*1966 and four new houses built on the site.

Bromborough

The Marfords was built in the mid c19. In 1850 it was occupied by George Edwin Taunton, a sharebroker. By 1885 Richard Hobson J.P. and family resided there. Richard, a cotton broker and a J.P. financed the local Church Institute, built in 1908, in memory of his wife, Eleanor. *The Marfords* was bought by Dr Barnardo's in 1936 (the previous owner being Samuel Mason Hutchinson, a flour miller, who was Lord Mayor of Liverpool in 1910-11) and was one of their homes until it was no longer suitable, closing in 1962. They let the building for a boys' Remand Home, but in 1976 the house was demolished. Barnado's gave eight acres of land to the local community and sold the other six acres for building.

Brookhurst, was situated on the south side of Allport Road, almost directly opposite *Bankdale* (*see next photo*) at the top of what became known as 'Fox's Hill'. In 1874 it was occupied by an American, HD Brandreth (of Brandreth's Patent Plaisters [plasters]). By 1880, Charles Bamford, provision merchant, had moved here; in that year he donated the bells for Bromborough Parish Church in memory of a son. At the outbreak of World War Two in 1939, Somerville Preparatory School moved here from Albion Street, New Brighton and it was still here in the mid 1960s. The building and its home farm were eventually demolished and the north end of Brookhurst Avenue now occupies part of the site.

Bankdale once stood on the North side of Allport Road almost opposite *Brookhurst* (*see previous picture*). In 1871 it was listed as *Dibbinsdale Bank,* but by 1889, during its occupancy by Henry F Fox, it had become known as *Bankdale*. Henry Fox must have been a notable character as the steep part of Raby Hall Road (the continuation of Allport Road) outside the site of *Bankdale* is still known locally as Fox's Hill. When the last occupant, James P Rudolf J.P., moved out in the late 1930s , the building was demolished. Housing was built there *c.*1970 with Barrymore Way now occupying part of the site. The Lodges to the former building are still standing, one in Dibbinsdale Road and one in Allport Road.

Robert's Garage is pictured in New Chester Road, Bromborough, with Allport Road off to the left, in 1933. Alfred Roberts had opened Central Garage, a converted barn at Bromborough Cross, in 1926 (*see page 51*) where he sold and repaired cycles and also had one petrol pump. He was very ambitious and with the financial help of a local gentleman, Mr Woodvine, he built a new garage *c.*1928 which is pictured above. The family house can be seen behind the garage. Locals thought he was ill-advised to site the garage there as there was then little traffic on this road. However, the business proved to be a great success and stayed within the family for over 50 years until it was sold in 1979.

Bromborough Golf Club was founded in 1904 by a local farmer, Mr Hassall, and a set limit of 100 members was soon reached. The first Captain was Squire Green. Lord Leverhulme was the first President and the land which formed the nine hole course was purchased by him from the Earl of Shrewsbury, as it was part of his Raby estate. During the First World War, the Club was closed and the clubhouse used as an auxiliary military hospital, seen above *c.*1916 with a group of Red Cross nurses. After the war the Club reopened and was extended to 18 holes in 1923. During the Second World War the Club was again requisitioned and an American Army Base constructed to house troops prior to the D Day landings. The only parts remaining untouched were the greens which were surrounded by barbed wire. It was not until 1949 that the club was able to reopen with the first captain being the present Lord Leverhulme. In 1969 the course was again reorganised due to the construction of the M53 Motorway. However, the Club benefited from the offer of Lord Leverhulme to make further old Hassall farmlands available, which provided an improved course. A new clubhouse was constructed in 1973 when it was found impractical to extend the original buildings.

A 1923 picture postcard depicts the red sandstone quarry which was on the opposite side of Allport Lane to where the Bromborough Methodist Church was erected in 1928. This must have then been an exciting 'play area' for local children. The Woodward family were listed as stonemasons and owners of the quarry from 1849 to 1915, when E Woodward was listed in a local directory as Quarry Owner, and it ceased being used in 1916. Many of the old Bromborough buildings pictured in this book were built with stone from this quarry. The quarry was eventually filled in with spoil from the construction of the Queen Elizabeth II Oil Dock at Eastham 1949–53; today the area is an unenclosed, pleasant grassy space crossed by public paths and surrounded by trees.

The half-timbered Council Offices on the left in Allport Lane, built c.1911, were demolished and replaced by the Civic Hall and Library building which opened 20 July 1973. The site between the Council Offices and the gable-end of the shops used to be the Council's yard but is now occupied by a supermarket. The shops on the right are still there today but the typical 1930s facia has been replaced with a straight roof-line.The shops trading in 1940 were from the right:- John Berry, Wine & Spirit dealer; Misses Mary & Priscilla Thompson, Confectioners; Hamlet Taylor, Greengrocer; Robert Thomas Valentine, Butcher; Alfred Lee, Pastry Cook and Miss Annie Millar, Chemist.

This picture postcard looking along Allport Lane towards The Cross was posted in 1931 and shows the shops on the left which stood on the site of *Manor House Farm* (*see page 54*) from the left - Malcolm Maynard's, Newsagent; The Monument, Sweets & Tobacco; Edna Hope, Confectioners and Irwins Grocers shop. Lily Southwood, Greengrocer and Samuel Allen, Butcher are on the right and to the left of the Cross is Sarah Marshall's sweet shop (*see page 56*) then RA Roberts' Central Garages, founded in 1925. Within a few years Alfred Roberts had built a garage with house alongside on the New Chester Road at the junction of Allport Road (*see page 49*) where the business remained in the family for over fifty years before being sold in 1979. Between Roberts and the lamp post is a small building which was Murphy's Taxi Office and is still there today and to the left is the entrance to Sheridan's Smithy (*see next picture*).

The entrance to the Sheridan's Smithy was between the barn that was to become RA Robert's Garage and the Church Institute (*see previous picture*). Both the Smithy and the *Smithy Cottage* were demolished in December 1982.

This, the third Church of St Barnabas at Bromborough, was built 1863/64 at the instigation of Rev E Dyer Green. The first Saxon Church survived until it was demolished in 1827/28 and a new Church built on the site. The tower and spire were added to the present Church in 1880. It was Rev E Dyer Green who also instigated Robert Rankin, occupier of *Bromborough Hall*, to pay for the Bromborough National Schools, seen on the left, which were inaugurated on 15 January 1869. Prior to that the school was housed in Village Road. The new school was built with materials from the demolished farm and cottage buildings which had occupied the site and also stone from the local quarry (*see page 50*). The school finally closed on 26 July 1983 but the building was opened as a village centre in 1985 and is still thriving today. Note the girl standing on the 'Big Stone', the glacial erratic still to be seen at that spot.

Bromborough Association Football Club team is posing for the photographer in the field they played on which was known as the Bradmoor. The Parish Church can be seen in the left background of this picture which was taken about the period of the First World War. This team played in the West Cheshire League and the other in Bromborough, Bromborough Village, played in the Bebington League. Both teams have disbanded and the new library was built on part of this field.

The *Royal Oak* is seen opposite The Cross c.1890 when Thomas Davies was the victualler. It was said to be one of Wirral's oldest public houses, dating back to the time of Charles I. The pub, which was owned by Birkenhead Brewery since the early part of this century, was not large enough for the increased trade and in 1958 its licence was transfered to the new *Royal Oak* situated across the road. All the buildings in this photograph are still standing except Hodgson's shop to the right which was demolished and an extension to the bank (*see page 55*) was built on the site.

To the right of the Village Cross can be seen part of the *White Row Cottages* on the East side of Village Road With many of the residents being employed at the Hall. They were demolished in the early 1930s. *The Royal Oak* (*see picture above*) can be seen adjoining WY Hodgson & Co's Grocery shop whose business was founded in 1877 in Tellett's former farmhouse. They had moved here by 1885, the previous owners being A & J Briscoe – millers, bakers & grocers. These two businesses, like many in the area, benefited from trade with the workers on the Manchester Ship Canal which opened in 1894. Miss Glover's sweet shop can be seen on the right.

Bromborough Cross, like most others in English villages, was the focal point for all the village activities and celebrations, as seen here for the Bromborough Coronation Festival 22 June 1911. The base and steps probably date back to late c13 with a new shaft and canopied head being added in 1874. The village market would be held within sight of the Cross, where buyers and sellers would trade and where farm labourers could be hired. *Manor House Farm,* seen in the background, stood in Allport Lane at its junction with The Rake. Built of sandstone the house dated back to at least 1676 which was the date on a stone house-plate found in the garden. The property was purchased by John Irwin & Sons, grocers, in 1928. The building was demolished and shops built on the site in Allport Lane (*see picture below and page 55*). Irwins were taken over by Tesco in 1960.

The 1925 Bromborough May Queen festivities, having started from the Village Cross, are seen proceeding down The Rake and are making their way to the Bradmoor. A horse-drawn butchers' cart is seen ahead of a mineral water cart followed by pony and traps. The bill board is advertising the *Bromboro News.* The farm buildings in the background formed part of *Manor House Farm* which stood at the junction of Allport Lane and The Rake (*see above and next page*).

Miss Glover's sweet shop (*seen on page 53*) has become a bank in this 1920s photograph which is looking down Allport Lane from The Cross. The building next door was demolished to make way for the bank extention (*see picture below*) and the three men on the right are standing outside Allen's Butcher's shop. The premises are now occupied by Muffs of Bromborough – an award winning local butcher and delicatessen.

Looking in the other direction from the picture on page 51, the then new bank building on the left replaced the old buildings seen above. The number 43 Birkenhead Corporation bus is a Leyland TitanTD2 which came into service in 1932 and was one of the first two diesel-engined buses in the Birkenhead fleet. It operated from Bromborough to Upton via Park Station and is seen standing outside Irwins grocery shop. This row of shops stand on the site of Old Manor Farm (*see page 54*).

Taken in the 1920s the building to the left of the Cross is the Church Institute built in 1908 for Richard Hobson in memory of his wife, Eleanor; then RA Roberts & Co's Motor & Electrical Engineers and Sarah Marshall's sweet shop to the right of the telegraph pole (*see page 51*). The buildings in New Chester Road on the right are seen in the next picture.

Looking down New Chester Road the single deck Birkenhead Corporation bus is a Leyland PLSC3 which entered service in 1927/28 being withdrawn in 1935. Behind the circular bench surrounding the base of the lamp post, which was a popular meeting place for locals (*see previous picture*), the wooden building was a temporary branch of the Midland bank. The buildings behind the bus are seen in the picture below and on page 56 and *Bromborough Hall* was behind the wall on the right.

A similar view to the previous picture looking down Bromborough Village Road (re-named after the by-pass was constructed in the mid 1930s), but taken in the 1950s, after the road had been widened in 1954. The temporary Midland Bank building has been replaced with a permanent one and *Bromborough Hall* has been demolished.

Looking down New Chester Road c.1930, H & B Storry's Chandlers shop, called *Allport House*, is seen on the left which was once *Tellett's Farmhouse* and has a datestone of 1685 (*see previous picture*). The farmyard and outbuildings, which were largely to the rear of the building have long since gone. The adapted farmhouse is still there today, housing a betting shop and hairdressing salon; the later building, to the right, is now a launderette.

The centre part of this building, on the west side of what was then the New Chester Road (Village Road), was Bromborough Post Office which was located here from about 1912; when this photograph was taken, *c.*1923, the Post Mistress was Sarah Hawkins who also sold glass, china and hardware, which can be seen displayed in the window. Misses Sarah and Annie Hawkins moved their business and Post Office facility to 23 Allport Lane in the early 1930s. Nowadays, the Post Office is located in High Street. The left side of the building with a crest between the windows stating 'County Constabulary' was the local Police Station with John Hadfield the then Constable. The Police Station is now sited in Village Road, moving there in the mid 1930s. Harry Wellings started Bromborough Paint & Building Supplies in the left side of this building in 1948; Tommy Lindsey's hairdressers was in the centre and the Hawkins family lived on the right. This property has since been demolished.

Bromborough Hotel is seen here in Village Road in 1911 when James McLeavy was the publican and the building had just been renovated. The hotel dates back to at least 1822 when it was known as the *Mainwaring Arms* with Thomas Humphries as the licensee. Then in 1850, when Mary Jones was the victualler, it was called the *Sportsman's Arms*. In 1896 another Mary Jones was listed as victualler by which time it had changed to its present name of *Bromborough Hotel*.

Stanhope House, seen here in the 1890s, is a three-storey sandstone building in Mark Rake at the junction of Village Road, dating back to 1693. The house was bought in 1937 by a local builder, Mr AH Boulton, who offered it in 1937 to the then Bebington Corporation in memory of his parents. The ground floor became the local library up to the 1960s. However, with little upkeep and vandalism the building was at the point of being demolished when Mr Raymond Richards of Gawsworth Old Hall restored the building to its full dignity. Today the whole building is occupied by a firm of accountants.

Bromborough Hall, which stood opposite the buildings on page 56, is seen here *c.*1920. It was built in 1638 by Bishop Bridgeman of Chester for his son, Orlando. In 1680, the Hall became one of the residences of the Mainwaring family; in 1851 it was leased to Robert Rankin, a Liverpool merchant; later the Dale family lived there and finally, in 1898, it was leased to Sir William Bower Forwood a Liverpool ship owner, who had been Lord Mayor of Liverpool in 1880. The Mainwaring family sold the estate to Lever Bros in 1905 but Sir William and family continued to live at the Hall until his death in 1928. The Hall was demolished in 1933 and the Bromborough by-pass cut through the grounds.

Old Hall Garage, seen here on the New Chester Road, stood opposite the east end of High Street. It was built on land purchased from Lever Bros 1934/36 on the Bromborough by-pass and advertised as official Morris and Standard Agents. A large bonfire was held in the field behind the garage to celebrate the Coronation in 1953. A new garage has recently been constructed on the site of the former one.

Although not in Bromborough, Spital Station, seen here looking in the Birkenhead direction *c.*1890, was used by many Bromborough residents as it was more convenient than Bromborough Station in Allport Road. This was an intermediate station on the Birkenhead to Chester railway - opening 23 September 1840. In 1907/08 the Italianate style station building on the left was demolished due to quadrupling of the line as far as Ledsham.

This photograph must have been taken prior to 1878 when the brick-built tower mill in the background, which had been erected in 1777 by Joseph Ellis, Miller of 'Bromborow', was considered unsafe and was blown up with gunpowder. The bricks from the old mill were used to build the row of cottages seen to the right in the picture below. Bromborough Water Mill, in the centre, is said to stand on the site of the mill mentioned in Domesday Book belonging to the Manor of 'Estham'. It was ideally situated standing at the head of a tidal creek running under red sandstone cliffs from the River Mersey and, as seen here, barges came right up to the mill at high water. The land, which had belonged to the Mainwaring family, was sold to Lever Bros in 1905. However, the construction of Lever's Railway Embankment in 1910 changed the nature of the site and the water mill was then unable to operate so an oil engine replaced the steam one.

Taken c.1928 from the same position as the picture above, on Spital Bridge, this photograph shows the tall chimney and engine house on the left which were built in 1835 for Fawcett Preston & Co who converted the mill for the use of steam. The tall sandstone building was the mill itself, dating back to c18 and the smaller building adjoining it, known as the 'old sack house' was probably late c17. To the right is the white c18 Miller's cottage then a sandstone barn and finally a row of brick cottages built 1878 with bricks from the demolished windmill. These were demolished in 1936. By 1949 all the pictured buildings had been demolished and the site sold. It is now occupied by a sewage pumping station.

Bromborough Pool

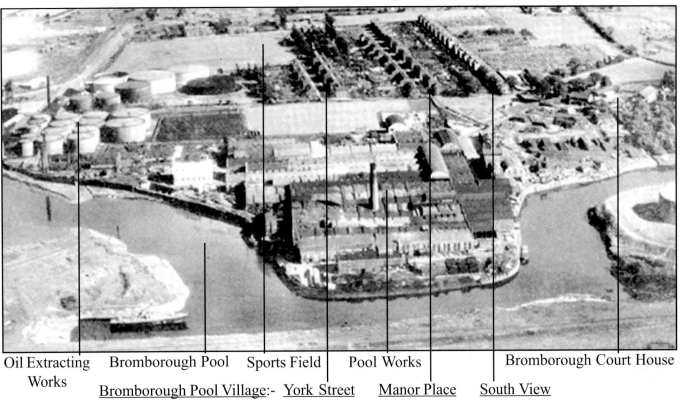

Oil Extracting Works   Bromborough Pool   Sports Field   Pool Works   Bromborough Court House

Bromborough Pool Village:-   York Street   Manor Place   South View

This aerial view, which was taken *c.1950*, shows the area covered by Bromborough Pool Village including Price's Village and 'Pool Works' factory in relation to the Bromborough Pool. The location of *Bromborough Court House* can be seen to the right (*see page 64*).

This etching, taken from The Illustrated London News dated 2 December 1854, depicts 'The Bromborough Pool Candle-Works – From The Mersey'. William Wilson had set up Price's Candle Works in Battersea (although there never was a Mr Price) and by 1854 had some 2,000 employees. As Liverpool was the main port for importing palm oil, the company decided on this 60 acre site with dock facilities and only four miles from Liverpool. Even before the factory was completed the company had started building a village for the workpeople as the nearest houses were two miles away.

Price's was bought by Lever Bros. 21 July 1922 from Burmah Oil Co., The Asiatic Petroleum Co. & Scottish Oils Ltd. This eliminated competition from Vinolia Soap. In 1937 the company divided into two parts with the Bromborough business joining the Unilever Group becoming known as Price's (Bromborough) Ltd – changing again to Unichema. The Battersea business retained the name Price's Patent Candle Company, became independent and devoted its activities to candles and lubricants.

For over a century *The Lodge* on the left, which was only ever occupied by three families - Craddock, Dodd and McDiarmid, guarded the only vehicular entrance to Bromborough Pool Village (the other entrance – for pedestrians and cyclists only, was in Dock Road South and was secured each evening at 10pm by the village policeman). The two white gates were closed once a year, with watchmen keeping vigil to preserve Prices' right of way into the village and factory. It is said that a toll of 2d was levied on residents requiring access after midnight! Notices were posted warning vagrants away from the village. The toll gates were dismantled during the Second World War with the metal parts being used to help the war effort and *The Lodge* was demolished in 1961/62 to allow for road improvements. The war memorial once stood to the right beyond the gates and the houses in the background are in Manor Place.

St Matthew's non-denominational Village Church of Bromborough Pool opened April 1890 in York Street opposite the VillageGreen. Designed to an early English syle, it was built of soft sandstone from the companies' quarry (now the site of Bromborough Pool FC's ground). Services were held in the factory for the first four years but moved to the school when it was built in 1858. It was the villagers who asked by petition for a Church to be set up. Alan Watson in his publication *Price's Village* describes how the life of the Church did not only centre around the building but revolved around the Chaplain, whose many duties included: running the Mothers Union; Lads' Guild; Lads' Bible Class; Boys' Club; Women's Bible Class; Senior and Junior Girls' Classes and a clubroom at the Chaplain's house. This gives an insight into the communal life of the village which gave the village its quality.

Looking down York Street, with a total of 32 houses, this was the first road in Bromborough Pool Village to be completed with the first resident moving in January 1854. Manor Place, parallel to York Street, was added in 1856 (*see aerial photograph on page 61*). Each house had an indoor WC with running water [unusual for that time] and a small garden front and rear as well as use of allotments. The first residents were key-workers from their Battersea factory who trained the local workforce. Initially there were few amenities with no school or shop, the nearest villages being New Ferry and Bromborough - both two miles distant in different directions. However, a Mrs Cowderay offered elementary education to children, using her front room at No5 York Street, until part of the factory was converted into a schoolroom and then the schoolhouse opened in 1858. The first village shop was opened in a garden shed and was to become the Industrial Provident Society founded in 1854, eventually being housed in the building seen on the right. Development of the village was completed in stages, depending on the company's finances.

This 1922 view of the 'Green' shows the chimney from Prices' factory in the background behind the cricket pavilion. This open space had been earmarked as the village recreation ground and as Prices' Battersea works had built up a reputation for their cricket the company seeded the cricket pitch here and contributed £10 towards cricket equipment and so the Cricket Club was founded in 1855 under the auspices of the Mutual Improvement Society. Two teams competed in the Merseyside Competition with members originally coming only from the village but later were also being drawn from other associated Unilever companies. More recently the club has merged and become Eastham Bromborough CC. The football club was founded in 1855 with matches being played here until the 1890s, when they moved to Eastham for a short period; then to a ground at New Ferry and in 1963 to the allotments on the south side of the village, which had been the site of the companies' quarry (*see page 61*). The land was converted into the pitch used today, with the club competing in the West Cheshire League since 1947.

This is *Court House Farm*, Pool Lane, which was built *c*.1680 by Henry Hardware of Chester, whose family were leading Puritans and afterwards Nonconformists. On the western side of the house once stood the moated Court House of the Abbots of St Werburgh which was accidentally destroyed by fire in 1284. Subsequently it was rebuilt and stood until the early c18 near the later Hardware building. This three-storied building, which stood within the old moat, lay on the south side of a large bend of the Bromborough Pool inlet and to the north west of Bromborough Pool Village. This site was on part of the land Levers bought between Bromborough Pool and Green Lane in 1905. One of the last farmers here was Bob Nichols whose name was carried on, in what is said to be the largest field in Cheshire and was known locally as 'Bobby Nicks'. The house was managed by Unilever Merseyside Ltd, who had let part of the building as flats to their employees but it was eventually demolished in 1969. The site was crossed by pipes until they were dismantled in 1999. There is little to suggest today that this important building once stood there, although much of the ancient moat remains.

The Stork Margarine Works are pictured in Stadium Road (so called as Lever Bros. planned to build a sports stadium here but developed the Bebington Oval instead). They were owned by Van den Bergh & Jurgens Ltd. when opened in 1932, replacing the older Planters Bromborough Margarine Works which had been set up by Lever Bros. in 1918 (they had taken Planters over in July 1915). This was due to a short supply of butter with the government keen to build up production of margerine during World War One. To this effect Lever Bros. built a new factory at Bromborough, going into production a few days before the Armistace in 1918. The decorative wooden pillars set against the front of the building originated from the bandstand at Port Sunlight, which was demolished *c.1934,* and the pillars re-used for decoration in front of the Stork Margarine factory. This photograph was taken in the 1950s when the Stork Margarine Works sign was lit up at night, as was the Stork on the roof. The building was demolished in 1957 and replaced by the present buildings.